Positive Th

30 Days Of Motivation And Affirmations: Change Your "Mindset" & Fill Your Life With Happiness, Success, & Optimism!

By: Robert Norman

© Copyright 2016 - All rights reserved.

In no way is it legal to reproduce, duplicate, or transmit any part of this document by either electronic means or in printed format. Recording of this publication is strictly prohibited and any storage of this document is not allowed unless with written permission from the publisher. All rights reserved.

The information provided herein is stated to be truthful and consistent, in that any liability, in terms of inattention or otherwise, by any usage or abuse of any policies, processes, or directions contained within is the solitary and utter responsibility of the recipient reader. Under no circumstances will any legal responsibility or blame be held against the publisher for any reparation, damages, or monetary loss due to the information herein, either directly or indirectly.

Respective authors own all copyrights not held by the publisher.

Legal Notice:

This book is copyright protected. This is only for personal use. You cannot amend, distribute, sell, use, quote or paraphrase any part or the content within this book without the consent of the author or copyright owner. Legal action will be pursued if this is breached.

Disclaimer Notice:

Please note the information contained within this document is for educational and entertainment purposes only. Every attempt has been made to provide accurate, up to date and reliable complete information. No warranties of any kind are expressed or implied. Readers acknowledge that the author is not engaging in the rendering of legal, financial, medical or professional advice.

By reading this document, the reader agrees that under no circumstances are we responsible for any losses, direct or indirect, which are incurred as a result of the use of information contained within this document, including, but not limited to, —errors, omissions, or inaccuracies.

Free membership into the Mastermind Self Development Group!

For a limited time, you can join the Mastermind Self Development Group for free! You will receive videos and articles from top authorities in self development as well as a special group only offers on new books and training programs. There will also be a monthly member only draw that gives you a chance to win any book from your Kindle wish list!

If you sign up through this link http://www.mastermindselfdevelopment.com/specialreport you will also get a special free report on the Wheel of Life. This report will give you a visual look at your current life and then take you through a series of exercises that will help you plan what your perfect life looks like. The workbook does not end there; we then take you through a process to help you plan how to achieve that perfect life. The process is very powerful and has the potential to change your life forever. Join the group now and start to change your life!
http://www.mastermindselfdevelopment.com/specialreport

Table of Contents

© Copyright 2016 - All rights reserved.

Legal Notice:

Disclaimer Notice:

Table of Contents

What Power Does A Quote Have?

What Is An Affirmation?

How Are Daily Affirmations Going To Help?

Chapter 1: Affirmations – Why They Work and How to Use Them Effectively

Chapter 2: Phase One – Days One Through Eight

Chapter 4: Phase Three – Days Fifteen Through Twenty-Two

Chapter 5: Phase Four – Days Twenty-Three Through Thirty

Chapter 6: What if it Doesn't Work?

Chapter 7: Positive Affirmations for Success

Chapter 8: Positive Affirmations for Good Health

Chapter 9: Positive Affirmations for your Career

Chapter 10: Positive Affirmations for Motivation

Chapter 11: Preparing and Using Your Own Affirmations

Summary

Thank you for purchasing my book "Positive Thinking: 30 Days Of Motivation and Affirmations: Change Your "Mindset" & Fill Your Life With Happiness, Success, & Optimism." Choosing this book is the first step to bringing positive thinking into your life, the next step is to follow the day by day instructions as they are listed in the book and watch your life transform before your eyes.

One of the most efficient ways you can improve your life is by simply thinking in a more positive way. This isn't anything new, and probably isn't something that you haven't heard before as it is one of the most common pieces of advice that is given. However, it isn't as easy as it sounds. In fact, it is one of the most difficult things you are going to do. If it were as easy as it sounds, we would be living in a world full of people who see the glass as being half full and people wouldn't struggle with mental health.

You are probably wondering, if being more positive is the most effective way to bring more happiness into our lives, why aren't more of us more positive? There are a few reasons why it is incredibly difficult to become more positive.

How We Think It Is, Is How It Is – It's easy to confuse what has happened in our past as what is going to happen in the future. What we fail to realize is that what happened in our past does not have to equal the future. If you believe that it does, then it does. But, if you believe it doesn't, then it doesn't. It's that simple.

Changing Our Mind Set Is Hard – to become more positive, it is going to require that you change the way you are currently thinking. Changing how you view things isn't easy. Throughout our lives, we are told that things are the way they are. At no point are we told that we have the power to change it. Today I am telling you; you have the authority to change your mindset and become more positive.

Lack Of Energy And Motivation – Changing the way we think isn't easy. It takes a lot of emotional energy. If you are stressed out by work and your personal life and aren't eating or sleeping well you aren't going to have the energy that is required to change how you think. This is especially true if you aren't sure how being more positive is going to benefit you on a personal level.

So how do you get that motivation? How do you learn what the benefits to becoming more positive are? That is where this book comes in. This book is going to provide you with thirty days of affirmations and quotes that are designed to bring more positivity into your life.

This book is going to have each day on its own page, so you aren't distracted by the next day's reading. The thirty days are separated into four "phases" and each phase is going to include a challenge for you to complete throughout that phase. None of these challenges are going to be very difficult, and they were all designed with the purpose of making you more mindful of your thoughts and how they affect you and your life. Each day is going to include a quote as well as an affirmation for you to say to yourself.

What Power Does A Quote Have?

You are probably wondering if reading a quote is going to be enough to change how you are thinking and turn you into a more positive person. The answer is a resounding yes. Quotes have the power to coach us when we can relate to the situation the quote is discussing. They are often inspirational and give us the faith we need to know we are capable of accomplishing something. With each quote that you are going to read in this book, you are going to take the time to think about how it relates to a situation in your life. There is always some truth found in a quote though it may not directly be your truth, it certainly can pertain to a circumstance someone you may know might be going through. Remember, sharing hope and encouragement can return to you and yield a wonderful outcome.

Quotes often subconsciously subject imagery. As you read a quote you often envision yourself in that statement. You can immediately see yourself as the reason that quote is being said. Since quotes are an excerpt from another source it has often led others to desire to read more from that author in the search for more understanding.

There are countless philosophers, writers, poets, spiritual, and religious sources to draw wonderful and meaningful quotes from. There is a quote for everyone and it fits every kind of situation. Quotes can be seen as an art piece able to be dissected in any way that the viewer sees, and that is what makes them so direct and personal.

What Is An Affirmation?

Being able to have a thought, an aspiration, a dream is something that every human being who has ever lived has had and is undoubtedly something that we all are entitled to. Having the ability to have a goal in your mind and say "I can really do this" is the seed of self-motivation. There are also times when you may have self-doubt and are questioning your own position in your aspirations. This is the time when you must persevere and confirm all of what you want. You can achieve this through allowing yourself to give affirmation into your life. An affirmation is something you are going to say to yourself to undo the negative self-talk that you are currently experiencing. You might think you aren't experiencing any negative self-talk, but chances are that on some level, you probably are. Negative self-talk covers everything from believing you aren't going to be able to accomplish something to not liking something about yourself.

You are going to say your affirmations to yourself at least twice a day for five minutes at a time. This means that you are going to repeat your affirmation repeatedly for that five minutes. Say your affirmation slowly and allow the words to sink into your mind and become a part of your everyday thinking. Keep in mind that your environment that you speak your affirmation in is very important. You want to be in a place that is peaceful or meaningful to you. You may have young children who are going to and coming in from school, you may have a million things to do while getting ready for work in the morning. These may not be the right times for your daily affirmations to be spoken.

By reading these quotes and affirmations daily, you are reminding yourself every day of all of the good in your life. Quotes and affirmations have the power to change our thinking and help us to see something in ourselves that we want to change or overcome.

How Are Daily Affirmations Going To Help?

There are some great benefits to getting daily inspiration as well as saying daily affirmations.

- You are going to be aware of your daily thoughts and words, which is going to reduce the amount of negative thoughts that are going to be able to enter your mind.

- The daily practice is going to help you to keep things in life in perspective. In the fast-paced life that we currently live in, it is easy to take the good things in life for granted, and even easier to focus on the bad things. Something as simple as an affirmation saying "I am healthy" in the morning is enough to remind you to be grateful for the good things in your life.

- The practice of daily affirmations and quotes can allow for you to gain mental freedom. You begin to move through the day differently. The things that use to be a bother to you are no longer seem too important. You might also begin to venture into new things that you never thought you would do.

- Daily affirmations are great for increasing how positive you are. When you are more positive, you are going to notice more of the great things that are happening in your life and welcome more blessings and gifts into your life.

- Like bees are attracted to flowers others will become attracted to you. As you become more positive and happy, other people are going to notice. You are going to find yourself helping others without even trying and seeing that is going to help you to stay even more focused. When you have the gift to be an inspiration to others you will continue to affirm your success.

When we can visualize our goals, you are a third of the way to achieving your dream. A vision is something that's internal and special. It is something that is personally given to you. While the destination may be in common with others your journey is specific and unique. There is no two journeys in life that are identical. When faced with achieving a goal no matter what it is you must have a few things that are parallel to you achieving your destination.

First, you must have a clear mindset of what you want. There would be a fault in your destination if you are not clear on exactly what you want to achieve. Secondly, you have to be sure that this is what you want. Being indecisive is a negative variable when trying to achieve a goal. Not being able to go through with anything because you are uncertain if you want to really do it is a waste of time. You must then be able to visualize your goal in its finalization. This is important, when you can see yourself being an entrepreneur, being a doctor, or having lost 50 pounds then this is where the destination becomes more vivid and clear. After doing that you must the go to work! It will be difficult at some point because hey, life happens, but you must be able to push through it in order to continue down your journey. There will be doubts, discouraging moments and sometimes people who will try and deter you from reaching your goals but YOU have to be the one who does not allow for them to take over.

Don't get discouraged if you struggle to eliminate the negative thoughts completely from your mind immediately, it's natural. Simply try to change the negative thought into a positive one. If you can't, just let the negative thought go, recollect your thoughts, and think about something else instead.

Are you ready to get started? Remember to start on day one and do one page a day until you reach the end. In thirty days, you are going to have undergone a complete mental transformation from negative and unhappy to being a positive, happy person on their way to success. Best of luck, enjoy the journey.

Chapter 1: Affirmations – Why They Work and How to Use Them Effectively

"Affirmations are our mental vitamins, providing the supplementary positive thoughts we need to balance the barrage of negative events and thoughts we experience daily." – Tia Walker

It would be so easy for us to toss positive affirmations aside as nothing more than new-age nonsense, a habit that is practiced only by those who are gullible. But there are too many success stories for this and, provided you use them in the right way, you will find that positive affirmations are incredibly powerful, a true aid to success and happiness throughout your life.

Unless you don't have the Internet or the television, you cannot have missed the strong and ever-growing popularity of positive affirmations. They are just about everywhere you look, even on pictures, cups and table coasters. But what are they exactly and why do they work?

What is an Affirmation?

An affirmation is the practice of thinking positively and of empowering yourself. They normally take the form, as you will see throughout this book, of short statements that you must repeat to yourself to create reality in your life. These affirmations are always in the present tense, never past and never future.

While cynical people may choose to write these off as having no meaning, as thoughts that we simply repeat to ourselves instead getting down to the work of making plans for action, affirmations actually play a very big part in the work that you do to mold the career that you want and, provided they are used in the right way, they can help you to get to your destination, taking the right route and with confidence. And, rather than being something we invented just recently, affirmations have been about for a very long time, conceived originally by a man in the medical profession

A Short History of Affirmations

The man who is responsible for affirmations is a French pharmacist and psychologist by the name of Emile Coue. Back in the early twentieth century, he noticed that, when he gave patients a potion and told them, at the same time, just how effective it was, he got better results than with those he said nothing to.

It was then that he realized our minds are constantly occupied by thoughts and that these thoughts became reality, a kind of autosuggestion when he told his patients to repeat these words every day – *"Every day, in every way, I am getting better and better"*. Throughout his work, Coue was responsible for achieving many cures, many of them remarkable, but he also failed in a way as well. He concluded that, if his patients could make an independent judgment about the affirmations they were saying, his methods would not work and his conclusion was that, for an affirmation to work, you have to truly believe it.

Why Not All Affirmations Work

That belief is one of the stumbling points of affirmations. Yes, you can say to yourself repeatedly, "my post-baby career is amazing" but, unless you actually believe that, deep inside of you and with all of your heart, it simply won't work.

You can choose a mantra and you can repeat it every single day but there is no way you can fool the very core of you and if you want your mantra to come true, you must have the deepest of true beliefs in it. Sadly, therefore many people fail with affirmations and I will talk more about this in a later chapter but, we tend to believe that our mantras must be ambitious otherwise there is no point. Dream a big dream or don't dream at all and that is not the way affirmations work.

It is perfectly okay to have a big dream, but when there is no realism in it then it can prove to be a case of 'your reach exceeding your grasp'. We must keep a realistic approach to our goals. Saying that "*I want to go into outer space next year*" and not having a single course on the fundamentals of space under your belt is an unrealistic approach to a big dream. When you have unrealistic goals you are subjecting yourself to vulnerability. If you are unsure of how to set realistic goals no need to worry, I will discuss them later on in this book.

We also make the mistake of looking for affirmations that someone else has come up with, that we can use for our own purposes without really making sure that they work for us. To show you how some affirmations are badly or poorly written, look at these:

- Saying to yourself, "*I am as thin as a supermodel and well-toned*" isn't going to work when what you see in the mirror is the baby weight you are struggling to shed and you haven't been anywhere near a gym in, well, forever.

- ☐ Saying to yourself, *"I am running the most successful multinational company"* won't work if your main way of filling your time through the week is sat down watching television.

- ☐ Saying to yourself, *"I am wealthy beyond everything I dreamed of"* won't work if you can't find the money to pay your bills and haven't treated yourself to any new clothes or shoes in months

There is a danger in picking an affirmation that doesn't fit with how you feel and that is that it can make you do the opposite of what you wanted. Instead of a feeling of empowerment and positivity, you end up throwing the towel in, thinking to yourself that where you want to be is so far away from where you are, and you'll never be able to get there so there really isn't any point in trying.

What do you do? Forget your affirmations, throw them all away and go back to how you were. That is absolutely the wrong thing to do. What you must do is pick the right affirmations, or write your own, and use them in the right way.

Finding the Right Affirmation

So, how do you pick the affirmation that is going to work for you? In a lot of ways, it is like a SMART goal:

- ☐ **S**pecific
- ☐ **M**easured
- ☐ **A**chievable
- ☐ **R**ealistic
- ☐ **T**ime-Related

First, your affirmation must not be vague. Saying something like, *"I have a fantastic career"* isn't really giving your subconscious anything to work with and it is too broad to generate any true conviction. It will also not help you to realize when you have achieved your goal. Instead, you should consider something that is near enough to your situation at the current time to be achievable and realistic. Then find or write an affirmation around it. A couple of examples would be:

- ☐ I enjoy what I do and I am truly appreciated for it
- ☐ I am on a journey that will help me run my own company

- ☐ I respond calmly to stressful situations

- ☐ I am confident and completely at ease in my job interview

These may be slightly above what you are feeling right now because they are describing something that you desire, not something that you cannot attain. They will also let you take the right action for you to achieve them and once you have done that, you move on and come up with a new affirmation for the next big step. Simply match your mantra to your progress, like taking a large project and breaking it down into smaller, more manageable projects.

You must have a sense of certainty of your affirmation, is it something realistic, smart and resourceful? If your affirmation is not achievable, is too ambitious, your core is not going to believe that you can achieve it and that means it will fail.

Create Your Own Personal Affirmations

So, what do you do? Affirmations do work if you use them properly and that means forgetting the one-size-fits-all approach. Yes, you can look for ideas for positive affirmations and, if you find one that fits your situation properly, use it. If not, adapt one or write your own. Tweak existing ones if you need to but make sure they genuinely work for you. <u>Remember:</u> Only **YOU** know what will work for **YOU.**

Chapter 2: Phase One – Days One Through Eight

"We first must think 'I can,' then behave appropriately along that line of thought." – Marsha Sinetar

Since this is your first phase, we are going to make your challenge an easy one. This challenge is something you need to accomplish every day, and not just for this week, but on throughout the entire thirty days.

This phase's challenge has been designed to help you be successful at becoming more positive. Making extra time in your day for new goals can be difficult to do. To help offset that, your challenge this week is going to be to get up a few minutes earlier.

Challenge – Phase One: Set your alarm fifteen minutes earlier than what you are getting up at right now. Use those fifteen minutes every morning to read through that day's affirmation and quote. Take your time reading the affirmation and quote and make sure that you read them more than once.

After you have read the quote a couple of times, close your eyes and think about what the quote means to you. Consider how the quote makes you feel and how you can relate to the quote. If how the quote makes you feel is negative, take a note of that and see if you can find a more positive way to frame your feelings.

Each day is also going to have some things that you can take into consideration to help you get started with the thinking process. As you consider each quote and affirmation, feel free to make notes and jot down any thoughts that you connect to them.

Write the affirmation down somewhere that you are going to see it throughout the day. Whether that means that you are going to email it to yourself, write it on a sticky note and place it on your computer or put it on your phone, make sure it is accessible and visible.

Keep three or four of the affirmations in this book together where you can recite them twice a day. You aren't going to want to have more than three or four to recite a day as this is going to create additional mental stress. Choose the ones that you feel apply the most to your life as the ones that you are going to recite to yourself. You can change which ones you are reciting each day as you wish to.

Day One

Quote*:* "You can achieve anything you want in life if you have the courage to dream it, the intelligence to make a realistic plan, and the will to see that plan through to the end." – Sidney A. Friedman

Affirmation*:* The power is within me. I learn from the past, live in the now and plan the future.

Some Things You Should Consider:

When you have courage, you empower yourself to go after something that you may not have any prior knowledge about. Courageous people have often become immortalized throughout history. Courage doesn't come only in the form of wars and battles but can come from personal situations. It takes courage to realize that there is something in your life that you want to change. It takes even more courage to come to the conclusion of beginning to take steps towards what you want to change. When you are courageous you are opening so many links to new opportunities and adventures. Let's be truthful, being courageous is not always easy. Sometimes it can be downright brutal, but it is necessary when the evolution of something is involved. Courage comes from some one having a made-up mind on a circumstance or a situation and finally saying "enough is enough." Only then does true courage come into play, and results are soon to follow.

Many people often correlate the words *intelligent* and *smart* together when in all actuality they are very different. A person can be smart but lack intelligence and a person can be intelligent and not so smart. Do not confuse the two words, you need both to become accomplished.

However, being intellectual is something that you are born with and being smart is something that you learn throughout life. When facing a new situation it is important to gather as much information that you can on the subject matter. This is called being educated, once you have gained education then you are able to apply what you have accumulated to whatever specifics are required. When you are smart you make the best of whatever kind of situation you are faced with. You give it your best and you are also giving your best to the people who are surrounding you. You are showing all of your best attributes: how you verbally communicate, the body language that you give, or your expressiveness. An intelligent individual is someone whose sense of awareness be it for environmental or internal stimulus is quickly absorbed.

Willpower is within all of us. Just like young children who are tempted to eat candy after they have been told not to. It is something that gives us the urge to have a persistent drive. Doing what we want to do whenever we want to do it. Although all of that can sound very empowering but to have an uncontrolled willpower can prove to be a problem when going through life.

Willpower and self-control work hand in hand. There are some things that we really want to do but then have to remove ourselves and our emotions from the situation and ask ourselves "Is this really good for me?" and then attempt to make the best judgment. The key to having great willpower is to have optimum self-control. We all need to practice having self-control as difficult as it may be it can and will keep you from setting your own self back. Self-control is also something that must be practiced over and over again for as you know temptations surround us all every day. The moment that you begin to feel like you are losing self-control is the time to take for personal reflection. Where do you want to be in life? Are the decisions you are making going to impact your goals in a negative way? If so, how should you go about changing your way of thinking to persevere in terms of your aspirations?

People do have differences when it comes to defining what being accomplished is. Some feel that being accomplished is having lots of money, having the "perfect" body or the best relationship. While there are so many definitions, only one has carried so much meaningfulness. It is that being accomplished encompasses the sense of success as a result of preparation and training.

While you are thinking about this quote and repeating this affirmation, think about the things in your life that you want to accomplish. Dreams that you haven't pursued because you feel like you won't accomplish them. Think about the challenges you have overcome in the past.

Say this affirmation like you mean it and believe it. Before you go to bed tonight, stand in front of the mirror and look yourself in the eyes. Repeat today's affirmation and tell yourself you are going to be a better person after these thirty days. Continue telling yourself that you are going to be a better person at the end of this thirty days.

Day Two

Quote: "Man often becomes what he believes himself to be. If I keep on saying to myself that I cannot do a certain thing, it is possible that I may end by really becoming incapable of doing it. On the contrary, if I have the belief that I can do it, I shall surely acquire the capacity to do it even if I may not have it at the beginning." — Mahatma Gandhi

Affirmation: I choose to find hopeful and optimistic ways to look at this.

Some Things You Should Consider:

At a certain point, we all should realize that we are our best advocate. There is no one that can do as much as you can do for yourself. When we have a strong belief that we are capable of doing anything with the right tools we can become unstoppable in this world.

When you are thinking about this quote, consider what you believe yourself to be. If you find yourself using negative words to describe yourself, try to replace as many as those negative ideas with a positive twist on them. If you still find difficulty blocking out those negative thoughts one thing I find helpful is to write down on one side of paper ALL of the things that you dislike or want to change about yourself and on the opposite side write ALL of the things you absolutely love about yourself. When you look at the things you dislike think about the things you want to change about them and how to go about that change. What are some things you need to cut out from your daily life to achieve this change? What is a realistic timeframe that you want to give yourself in order to ensure an achievable destination?

Anytime you are faced with a struggle, repeat the affirmation above. Whether this is a personal struggle, a work struggle, or a financial struggle, this affirmation is going to help you through it. After you have repeated this affirmation when you are struggling for a while, you are going to find yourself naturally looking for a more optimistic approach to a situation without having to give it any thought.

Day Three

Quote*:* "Once Your Mindset changes, everything on the outside will change along with it." – Steve Maraboli

Affirmation*:* I clearly see the beauty of life that flourishes around me

Some Things You Should Consider:

While you are thinking about this quote, consider how you look at things. Consider whether you are the kind of person who sees beauty in things or notices the ugliness around them. If you are the kind of person who sees the ugliness, think about how you can see the beauty around you instead. Begin to empathize to the conclusion that there is beauty and wisdom in every situation, whether good or bad. There is always something that we can take away from situations, even if it is not our own.

Having a highly effective mindset makes the best out of any and every kind of situation. It enjoys being in that open space, that present feeling and moment. When you have a passion for something it's almost impossible not to put all of your heart into it. Having a, well, effective mindset will connect that inner drive and the physicality needed to make it your goals real. When your mind is effective the small things that use to be bothersome are no longer. You begin to have a filter of what is important in life and what isn't. You will be able to remain focused on the things that are important along with having the discipline to carry them out. With the effective mindset, you hold the key to opening any of the doors that have been closed in your past, present, and future.

You may ask where or how to start building this *effective mindset*? Well, simple, you can start right now. There are a few ways to begin to build a healthier mindset. To begin, when we can think positively and are able to filter out all of the bad emotions from the past we can then begin to build a healthy mindset. By identifying your negative thoughts and feelings through having awareness. There are tons of cognitive awareness exercises out there that can assist you with this. Once you have an awareness of your thoughts then you can move on to the art of expression.

Expressing the thoughts that we have, whether happy, sad, mad or all in between are extremely important of having thoughtful awareness. By all means get creative. You can journal, dance, paint, scream, meditate or really anything that is a healthy gateway for you to express yourself and everything that might be bottled up on the inside. The moment that you begin to think negative thoughts is the time to refocus your thoughts and put your attention on the positive things about you or the positive things going on around you. Lastly, use your imagination! Imagery is so important in everyday life and it plays such a huge role in the way that we perceive the world. Try imagining yourself in a better place be it physically, financially, emotionally or mentally.

While you go about your day today, consider all the amazing things that are around you. From the flower growing in the garden to the bird flying overhead, there is beauty in all things, when you can see the beauty in these things you are going to be able to accomplish more.

Day Four

Quote: "The true secret of happiness lies in taking a genuine interest in all the details of daily life." – William Morris

Affirmation: For me, happiness is a journey, not a destination. I have been blessed with happiness, and my journey is endless.

What motivates you? Take a few minutes to really evaluate your answer. Do you get out of the bed because you have to, want to or need to? When you are on your morning, mid-day, and evening commutes, are you satisfied with what you are doing? What is it you are doing all of this for? When you are faced with these questions and you have all negative answers then it is time to re-evaluate what is keeping you in order to be doing the same things that are bringing you displeasure.

To be quite frank, life is too short to be doing something that you are not happy doing. In the terms of occupation, there are thousands if not millions who absolutely hate the occupation that they are currently in. The saving grace is that can be *changed*. You do not have to stick to a job that you do not love, while it is a great idea to have a backup plan before just putting in a resignation letter, there is nothing that makes you stay somewhere where you are not fulfilled.

When seeking motivation you should always take into consideration what it is that *you* want. Motivation should not come from someone else, it should come from you. When we are truly motivated to do something we withhold all prejudices and give it 100% every time and we are purely happy to do it.

Some Things You Should Consider:

The greatest journey that we all will ever be on is a simple word called *life*. Consider the parts of your day that bring you the most happiness. Is it when you wake up in the morning? Going for a quiet walk on a hiking trail? Drinking some delicious coffee? What is it about those parts of your day that make you happy? Think about the things that are all around you during those parts of the day. Consider the people, the noise levels, the smells, tastes and anything else that is within your surroundings. Take note of all of those details and commit them to your memory. These details will help you retain the good feelings associated with those experiences and remind you that at that specific moment in time there was a moment of bliss.

Day Five

Quote: "Happiness lies in the joy of achievement and the thrill of creative effort" – Franklin D. Roosevelt

Affirmation: Happiness is a choice. I base my happiness on my accomplishments and the blessings I've been given.

Some Things You Should Consider:

"He makes me happy."

"She makes me happy."

Have you ever heard anyone say those lines? My guess would be absolutely. In some form or another, we have always tried to associate our own personal happiness with the involvement of something or someone outside of our own self. This is not how happiness is developed or executed. The idea of having to chase after the emotion of happiness, an emotion that comes from nowhere but within, has been the downfall of so many people and has easily contributed to seeking validation from others. One must then ask themselves, "What is needed for me to be happy?" Take a minute or two and ask yourself what you think is needed in order for you to be happy.

Understand that no one can make you happy, though there are experiences that bring the emotion of happiness into margin but it's only received if you are open to the delivery. True happiness is personal and direct. Consider the things you have done in your life that make you happy. Think about the people in your life, and the goals you have accomplished that contribute to bring about your happiness. Realize that even when you weren't successful, the excitement of trying brought you happiness as well. There are going to be failures throughout life's journey, and that's okay, but it is up to you to disallow or allow for them to have a direct impact on you and how you are continuing throughout life.

Anytime you find yourself feeling unhappy with the hand life has dealt you, repeat the affirmation above and remember, happiness is a choice.

Day Six

Quote: "Progress is impossible without change and those who cannot change their minds cannot change anything" – George Bernard Shaw

Affirmation: I have been given endless talents which I begin to utilize today.

Some Things You Should Consider:

Progress is often understood as a business term, while it is most suitable for any business person to use in their endeavors it is a term that should be used in self-motivation and self-help. Having progress means that you have started from somewhere and you are advancing into something grander. Progress is the motion in-between ground zero and the finalization of a goal. In order to have progress, you must have productivity. What are you doing in your day to day living that is showing a direct progression to your goals and achievements?

If you find your answer to be in the negative aspect then my suggestions would be finding and applying steps to progression. Some of the steps may include:

-Know what makes *you you*. What do you do well? What are some of your favorite things to do on your down time? What are some things about your life that you want to change?

-Create a plan and know how to manage what your goals are. When you know what your goals are you create different strategies to help you strengthen those pieces of your life that will make you getting your goals.

- Be aware of what your setbacks are. When you are aware of the bad habits you practice you realize how much of it is a part of your life.

Ever hear the quote *"You are what you eat"*?, well here's another one for you to remember *"You are what you think"*. If you want to progress towards a happier life, you are going to have to change how you are thinking about things. This isn't as hard as it seems. While you are thinking about this quote, consider opinions or habits you have that you are unwilling to change. While thinking about them, are there any of these things that have proven to have a negative outcome? If so, is it something you can be comfortable living with for the rest of your life?

Anytime you find yourself in a situation that cannot be solved in the usual way, think about the affirmation above and remember that you are capable of change, if you just utilize your talents and find a new solution. Interpersonal change usually doesn't happen overnight and it may not even happen over a week, it takes time so don't rush.

Day Seven

Quote*:* "Don't rely on someone else for your happiness and self-worth. Only you can be responsible for that. If you can't love and respect yourself – no one else will be able to make that happen. Accept who you are – completely; the good and the bad – and make changes as YOU see fit – not because you think someone else wants you to be different." – Stacey Charter

Affirmation*:* I love and respect myself as I am.

Some Things You Should Consider:

This society has proven to be a place where being accepted by others should be the number one priority of the day. We put out everything we do on social media. We dress to impress! We try and keep up with the *"Who's who.."*. Why? While you are thinking about the quote above, consider how much you rely on other people to validate you. Are you confident in who you are, or do you need other people to give you positive affirmations to feel like you are worthwhile?

Only you can make you happy. No one in this world has the capability to do that. Seeking validation from others only allows for them to gain control and for you to lose control. It shouldn't matter what others think of you. Be the best you that you can be and anyone else's opinion should fall irrelevant, especially if it is negative.

The world we live in is all about representation, how a person presents them self is the number one judgment of character by others. The way you dress, the way you speak, or the way you look has a direct impact on how others will treat you. This is an unfortunate reality for many people, especially as young children are being more and more impacted of the idea of "image" and are sometimes willing to go to extremes to have their "image" protected. Self-esteem for adolescents and adults alike are often tangible according to our interactions with others.

When you have good self-esteem you have good self-values. When a person has good self-esteem they have a wonderful collective opinion about themselves - how they look, how they speak, their style and everything else! They view themselves as nothing less than great and they don't allow for others beliefs or opinions to impact them in a negative way. Your confidence level will increase drastically and you will find yourself being more comfortable and open with new opportunities and adventures. When you have high self-esteem you demand respect from others and give respect to others all because you have the highest respect for yourself. You also have true freedom and can openly and happily be yourself.

If you are struggling with having high self-esteem then there are some practices that you can try to heighten those emotions. You can begin with encouraging and complimenting yourself. Whenever you have made a mistake forgive yourself and forgive the people who have done wrong to you. I know that this may be very difficult but when we allow the hurt and pain another person has caused us to be unforgiven we are giving our power to that situation and this can be very draining to the mind, body, and spirit.

"The greatest thing in the world is to know how to belong to oneself."

-Michel de Montaigne, The Complete Essays

Having self-worth and self-values are essential in having a high self-esteem. When you have high standards about what you allow to enter into your life and your mind, you have the ultimate control on how situations cycle. If you know that there are some people in your life who tend to be a bit on the narcissistic side and they tend to bring you down then it will be easier to cut them out of your inner life when you have raised your standards. We should never settle for anyone or anything that goes directly against what we feel we deserve and our on moral character.

There are two types of influences: good and bad. The difficulty comes when we are naturally given the gift to have freedom of choice. The closer something is to you the greater of an influence it will have, if allowed. It is always a good idea to surround yourself with positive influences. These can really be in great variation as we are all drawn to different things. The key to being well influenced is to keep the bad influences far away! It is sometimes difficult to avoid the presence of a bad influence because they are indeed everywhere, but the wonderful news is that a bad intention sticks out like a sore thumb. *Misery loves company,* and it will do anything to have others join the party. If you are wise enough you can see someone who has a toxicity that would not be good for you to be around. When you are aware of this then it is easy for you to remove yourself from that situation.

Say this affirmation to yourself as often as you can, until you truly believe it. You cannot become more positive, happier or successful if you don't first love, respect and accept yourself for who you are.

Day Eight

Quote*:* "Work hard for what you want because it won't come to you without a fight. You must be strong and courageous and know that you can do anything you put your mind to. If somebody puts you down or criticizes you, just keep on believing in yourself and turn it into something positive." – Leah LaBelle

Affirmation*:* Giving up is easy, and always an option so I will delay it for another day.

Some Things You Should Consider:

Many things that come easy usually are not all that legit. If you ever recall getting a great deal on something and then after just a few uses it begins to give you some problems and soon after just doesn't work out altogether. That is a wonderful example of things that are cheap aren't necessarily good. There is the triangle often used by builders and designers, you can have something good, fast, or cheap. The trouble is you can only choose two of those options. If its good and fast, it won't be cheap. Cheap and good, it won't be fast. I think you're getting my point. So it is for going through life and climbing to your goals and aspirations. There is a lot of hard work that is required in order to get to a destination, sometimes decades worth. You have to be real with yourself and ask if that is something that you are okay with, being in something for the long haul because that is what you truly want.

When we have worked hard for something the passion is slowly kneaded into the pathway and we begin to have an appreciation for not only the hard work that we have done, but we appreciate ourselves even more for going through it. This increases our self-worth and it is such a great feeling. Remember that hard work never goes without being rewarded in the end. Whether your reward is something of the physical world or emotional, hard work pays off.

We must remember to teach others the value of hard work, especially our youth. It is important for them to know that nothing in life is promised and that there are sacrifices that must be made at some point in their lives. Equipping them with the knowledge of hard work will help them in so many ways.

Do not forget to be your biggest motivator, nothing will ever get done in your life unless you make it up in your mind that you need it and want it to come to pass. Anytime you find yourself struggling to motivate yourself to do something, say the affirmation above out loud. Remember, real strength shows itself when you don't quit, and you see something through to the ending. Not only does it build strength but it also builds character and many more wonderful attributes to you own self.

You have made it to the end of the first phase. Congratulations for making it this far. Consider how your thoughts have changed in the last week. Are you beginning to see things in a more positive way? Are you finding that you are happier and feeling more fulfilled?

Success Story – Thomas

"There is nothing in the world that I cannot achieve when I have the courage to believe."

— *Chiara Gizzi*

My name is Thomas, I am not quite 50 yet and I have been using positive affirmations for more than 20 years, almost constantly. Sometimes they have taken my life over and have delved into my pursuits in the biggest ways possible but to me, this is a good thing. Affirmations have given me the opportunity to transform myself in the most positive ways and have helped me on my way to accomplishing many goals.

It all began when I started to use affirmations to improve my confidence levels. When I started, I was 17 years old, shy, didn't find it very easy to make friends and I would as good as run from a girl! Within just a few days of using affirmations, I began to see a major difference in my thoughts, about how I saw myself, how is thought about happiness, my self-esteem, and positivity. Over the following weeks, everything changed for me and I was hooked – affirmations became my life. I was more outgoing and confident than I had ever been before, I found it easier to make friends and started socializing – and I started talking to girls!

This was just the start though and over the next 20 or so years, my day has begun, without fail, with 5 minutes of positive affirmations and, every day, the last thing at night, I repeat those affirmations into the bathroom mirror. Not a day has passed when I have not done this and the transformation has been remarkable.

What did I use affirmations for? Just about anything you can think of. They helped me to lose weight and start taking exercise on a regular basis. They pushed me into working hard at running and at sports. I used them to help me in my hobbies, to boost myself when I was down and to get the right mindset for running my real estate properties and my businesses. I also used them as a way of helping to boost my personal relationships and live life.

After spending the last 20 or so years running my own businesses I have now been able to take early retirement although I do keep my hand in with some business interests and personal projects. And I still do my affirmations, every single morning and night. Throughout my life, throughout all the changes, the ups, the downs, affirmations have been there for me and they can be there for you too.

Chapter 3: Phase Two – Days Nine Through Fourteen

"Thousands of candles can be lighted from a single candle, and the life of the candle will not be shortened. Happiness never decreases by being shared." – Buddha

You've made it to phase two! How did you do over the last week? Take a moment to consider how you did with the first challenge so far. Do you feel that starting your day with a quote and affirmation changed how you approached your day? Consider how you are feeling daily. Would you say that you can feel yourself becoming progressively more positive?

At this point, getting up a little earlier each day should be becoming a habit and a normal part of your routine. Remember that you are going to continue getting up early and committing that time to reflecting on the quote and daily affirmation of the day throughout the rest of the thirty days. You should also have a few affirmations that mean something to you that you are saying each day.

This phase's challenge is based on the quote above. Sharing happiness is a great way to bring more happiness to you, and when you see yourself bring happiness to others, you will be amazed at how great it makes you feel.

Challenge – Phase Two: Your challenge this phase is to spread a little happiness every day. This can mean anything you want it to. You can take a minute out of your day to call someone who you know would appreciate hearing from you. You can take a minute to thank the grocery store clerk for being kind. It could also mean surprising someone with a cup of coffee or a treat. Any form of gratitude or positivity is going to go a long way towards bringing happiness into other people's lives. When you see how happy you can make others, you are going to feel happier as well.

The reason that you feel happy when you make other people happy is that we can empathize the emotions that we observe in others. In the 1960's a Dutch Scientist, Christian Huygens discovered that if he hung multiple pendulums on the wall, they would all end up swinging in perfect synchrony. This proved to be true even if he set them in motion at different times. This happens in human beings as well. You have probably noticed that when someone is in a bad mood, that bad mood can be passed on to others. The same is true for happiness.

By spreading happiness to others not only do you gain the same emotion but they also have to capacity to now spread it to others and before you know it there is an overflow and what seems to be an endless chain reaction of happiness.

Day Nine

Quote: "There is only one way to happiness, and that is to cease worrying about things which are beyond the power of our will." – Epictetus

Affirmation: Happiness is my birthright. I choose to be happy, and I deserve to be happy.

Some Things You Should Consider:

While you are thinking about the quote above, consider all the things that you are worried about that are sacrificing your happiness. Is there anything you can do to control those things? Or are they beyond your control? For the things that are beyond your control, consider what you can do help reduce your worry about the things that are beyond your control.

Imagine a bag on your back, this bag holds every situation you ever have worried about; think on how heavy that bag is now? Is it just about to weigh you down? When we worry and continue to hold on to emotional baggage we are putting tremendous tension and weight on our mind. When our minds are down we are incapable of working to our fullest potential. I know, it is easier said than done, but when we worry about things that are out of our control it begins to control everything about us. We end up not functioning so well and this can then jeopardize our health and wellbeing.

The number one killer of humans is stress and the diseases brought about by stress. Stress is like a leech that feeds on every part of the human. It feeds on our minds, our bodies and our spirits. Fortunately, this can be managed through lifestyle alterations. Proper diet, expression, and exercises for the mind and body do wonders for someone who is trying to eliminate the feeling of stress. If there is a situation or a job that is more stressful than enjoyable and you find that it is too much, my advice would be to find something else that brings you peace and joyfulness.

Anytime you come across a situation that is decreasing your happiness, repeat the affirmation above. Remember, you deserve to be happy, and you can make the choice to be happy.

Day Ten

Quote*:* "It's not the events of our lives that shape us, but our beliefs as to what those events mean." – Tony Robbins

Affirmation*:* I always spot opportunities and utilize them. New doors are always opening for me.

Some Things You Should Consider:

Reading the above quote, can you think of some times in your life when you felt that you were being shaped by the things that were happening around you? What was shaping you, was it the event itself or how you were reacting to the event?

Many people consider themselves to be a victim of circumstance when it is an internal decision to allow the circumstance to define them. How can you change how you are viewing those circumstances?

Bad things are going to happen, but it is what you do once the bad thing has happened that counts. You just miss a flight to an important event, what do you do? Do you just quit and return home or do you try and reconcile the problem? There are always going to be moments in life when you think to yourself, "Can anything ever go right in my life?". The answer is yes but you have to also realize that bad things are a part of life and there is no way of getting around it. You have to just take things as they come to you and handle them in the most positive way you possibly can. If not, then you will shut yourself out of personal growth and opportunities.

There is also something called the Law of Attraction which an entire book can be written on but I will sum it up a little. When we put out the thought that something bad is going to happen then we are holding up a sign for all of the bad events that we are thinking about to come directly into our midst. We have to watch how we think and what we think. Some of the bad thoughts we have are a gateway for them to become our living reality. Whenever you think about something bad that is going to happen to you try are redirect your thoughts into a positive one.

For example, instead of saying *"I am going to get into a wreck."* Try saying something like, *"I am going to have a safe and wonderful drive."* This sends out the energy of attracting a good and safe journey versus attracting destruction and discord.

The above affirmation is a great one when you feel as though you are being limited by your circumstances. New opportunities are always opening themselves up to you, and there are always new opportunities for you to explore.

Day Eleven

Quote*:* "Action is the foundational key to all success" – Pablo Picasso

Affirmation*:* I am solution oriented. All problems are solvable.

Some Things You Should Consider:

When you consider the quote above, remember that the foundation of anything is the most important thing. When you are building a house, the house is only as strong as the foundation. The quote tells us that actions are the foundation for success. If you aren't taking any action, you aren't going to accomplish any success.

Action sometimes requires sacrifice. If your goal is weight loss then you have to watch how much and what you consume on an 'around the clock' basis. Sacrifice is not an easy thing especially when you are used to doing something you like or love. However, if you have a goal you're striving to achieve whether it's health, financial, or personal sometimes there will be huge sacrifices that must be made.

If you have felt as though you are stuck in a rut recently, and feel as though there is no way to move forward in your life, this affirmation is exactly what you are going to need to help you through it. Repeat this affirmation to yourself as often as you can. Remember, if you are looking for the solution, you are going to find it.

Recall earlier in this book when I stated that there would be some keys on how to build realistic goals. It is very important to set realistic goals for yourself, to promote healthy endurance and strive. Here are a few points to keep in mind when setting a realistic goal:

    1. Keep a visual representation of your goals. When we see something with our eyes multiple times it begins to make a fingerprint in our mind and this is very helpful when it comes to affirmations. You can write on whatever you like, a mirror, the wall, make a screensaver on your phone or computer, on poster board. Pretty much anything that you will see multiple times a day.

    2. Having smaller goals within a larger one. This helps to keep you motivated and moving in the right direction. Set up small milestones on your journey.

    3. Keep your goals uncomplicated. Be specific and upfront. State how you are going to go about achieving your goal.

Example:

<u>Make Better Grades</u>　　　　vs.
<u>Make Better Grades By</u>

Studying 30mins 4X Daily

Going to Study Sessions

Asking Specific Questions

    4. Measure your progress. If your goal is an increase in financial gain, see how your track of expenses have declined or inclined over all of your income.

When we take action on our goals we are adding the nutrient that is required for our dream to take root and grow. Actions are something that can be both voluntary and involuntary. When you put forth a good action then you will involuntarily receive action back. You may have the question of how to take action? The first thing is to have a reality check. What is your mindset focused on at the present time? You have to reconnect yourself with your thoughts and feelings. Once you have done that set your priorities in line. If you are in charge of governing over something or others then you have to be accountable and make yourself available. You then must hold yourself responsible for your actions and the outcome of your situation. You are the mastermind here and you are ultimately in control of how your life will and does play out. Set your own standards and principles on how you want things to go and try your best to not stray away from it. Lastly don't be too serious, when we are hard on ourselves or others it tends to take the enjoyment out of the circumstance. No one wants to be around someone who is always controlling and can never seem to lighten up.

These are all some positive ways to begin to take action in your life and your career. These things will assist in building great characteristics and moral.

Day Twelve

Quote*:* "Optimism is the faith that leads to achievement. Nothing can be done without hope and confidence." – Helen Keller

Affirmation: I am confident, and I am capable. There is no challenge I cannot overcome.

Some Things You Should Consider:

What is your definition of hope? What are some of the things you feel you are the most confident in? As the quote states about nothing in life can be done if we are not hopeful and confident. The whole idea behind wishing is the thought that hope and strong desire will bring whatever you want right into our lives. A wish is given usually when the situation seems very unpredictable and unobtainable. Hope is the belief that something can certainly happen, it is faith.

We have to believe in what we dream of, there is nothing more important in building ourselves up and moving throughout life. Empowerment of what you want through hope and optimism is what will keep you motivated and your dreams fresh.

Think about the situations that you are the most optimistic. What are the times that you are the most confident that you are going to be able to achieve your goals? What situations are you the least confident in?

When we have high confidence it empowers us to be our best, do our best, and think our best.

Some may experience a heightened sense of euphoria and adrenaline.

Whenever you are in doubt of your abilities, repeat the affirmation above. Place it next to your bathroom mirror, seeing it on a regular basis is going to help you believe it even more. Of all the affirmations that we have gone over this far, this is the one that you need to believe in the most.

Day Thirteen

Quote: "To carry a positive action, we must develop here a positive vision – Dalai Lama

Affirmation: I am going to help others. I have enough happiness inside me to share.

Some Things You Should Consider:

When you read the quote above, what is the very first thought that comes to your mind? Can you think of a time when you were expecting a negative outcome and it came true? What about a time when you were expecting a positive vision and the positive vision can true? Often, when you can envision the outcome being positive, you are more likely to get that positive outcome.

There is some truth to the laws of attraction, and we can sometimes be our worse enemy. People often expect the worst in a foreign situation and tell themselves that they are expecting the worst, so they shouldn't be disappointed when it happens right? However, they are still just as disappointed when their negative vision comes to fruition. Don't get caught up in that trap. When you think negative things are going to happen, they are more likely going to happen. Instead of thinking the worst out of a situation you are faced with try turning it around into a happier situation, think of something beautiful you can take away from it.

Having optimism through your everyday existence is what allows you to keep an open mind and an open heart. Believing in something far from what you can see gives you the inspiration to keep moving forward.

How are you doing on this phases' challenge? Are you finding it easy to bring happiness into other people's lives? If you are finding the challenge to be difficult, repeat the above affirmation to yourself. There is happiness inside you, and when you choose to share it with others, it comes back to you tenfold.

Day Fourteen

Quote*:* "You'll never find a rainbow if you're looking down" – Charlie Chaplin

Affirmation*:* I am kind, I am loving, I am happy.

Some Things You Should Consider:

Take time to think about what the quote above means. Think about a goal that you are trying to reach. Are you on the right path to meet that goal? If you aren't on the right path to reach your goals, you are never going to get to them. Take some time to analyze where you are in life and where you want to go. What changes can you make?

It is important to remember that no matter what kind of journey you are on you have to ensure yourself and make the most important person in your journey yourself. When there are rough patches in life you can feel alone, sad or like you aren't getting anywhere but know that after every dark storm comes wonderful sunlight.

Be inspired by the things that surround you. Anything and everything that we come in contact can have some type of meaning to it.

Sometimes things can come into our life for a reason and a season and it is up to us to recognize it and take what we need from it. There are many lessons that can be learned in every moment of the day.

No matter how far you are from the path you want to be on, you can still be happy with where you are. Remind yourself that you are a kind and loving person. Happiness is a choice you can make. If you aren't happy at this moment, only you can change that. Repeat the affirmation above and remind yourself of all the reasons you have to be happy.

Success Story – Whitney

"All is well. Everything is working out for my highest good. Out of this situation, only good will come. I am safe." – Louise L. Hay

My name is Whitney and, in the middle of the eighties, I was given a book, a book that I still must this day. My parents had been divorced for a few years and, although things were good, it was tough at a time when divorce want really all that common. A friend of my mother gave me this book, the Rainbow Heart Book, called "You Can heal Your Life" by Louse L Hay. And I must say that, since that time, my life has been one hell of a journey!

This brand-new book seemed to fit with me, being the kid of divorced parents at my school. Every exercise that was in it, I savored, just to get to know every different aspect of the me that I am. I wanted to be a better person, more accepting, more whole and I learned that I was a loving person, a lovable person and that I was loved, not just by me but by the entire universe – and I still am to this day.

Out of all the techniques in this book, the one that inspired me the most and has stuck with me is affirmations. It is these that I thank for the fact that I became a happy teenager, a confident one, one who was happy to be herself and not trying to be something others wanted me to be.

For me, an affirmation is everything and anything that I think, that I say, that I believe, experience and feel. Affirmations have become me, they reflect me and they are me.

So many people use negative self-talk and this is what drives their affirmations, drawing them into negativity that they really didn't want. It started like this for me but I learned to move my focus and use my affirmations for a more positive life and it is these positive affirmations that have seen me through many an uphill struggle.

When I was in my twenties, my dad passed on, completely unexpectedly and that changed my whole life forever. I got stuck in a grief rut – Í release myself as I do in each moment, free of self-judgment"

Later on, in my twenties, I was diagnosed with cancer and, as it does with just about everyone who is diagnosed, it stole my breath, it stunned me. I stumbled through wondering why this was happening, what had I done? At this point, my affirmations became passionate – "I am living my life to the full, treasuring every single day as it comes"

When I was in my thirties, I became unfulfilled with my job, I wasn't happy or satisfied with what I was doing. I felt as if I was overworked, ill because of stress and burned out. My affirmations changed – Í am living my purpose in life, engaging my Sacred Gifts for the healthy benefit of me and others around me"

Today, I am that happy smiling person I was back in twelfth grade and I put that down to my belief in affirmations and the fact that I have made them a part of my daily life, especially the most important one of all – "I am truly grateful"

You are halfway done!

Congratulations on making it to the halfway point of the journey. Many try and give up long before even getting to this point, so you are to be congratulated on this. You have shown that you are serious about getting better every day. I am also serious about improving my life and helping others get better along the way. To do this I need your feedback. Click on the link below and take a moment to let me know how this book has helped you. If you feel there is something missing or something you would like to see differently, I would love to know about it. I want to ensure that as you and I improve, this book continues to improve as well. Thank you for taking the time to ensure that we are all getting the most from each other.

Chapter 4: Phase Three – Days Fifteen Through Twenty-Two

"You cannot change what happens to you but you can control your attitude towards what happens to you, and in that, you will be mastering change rather than allowing it to master you." – Brian Tracy

You are still coming back every day and reading another page in this book, and you have made it to phase three.

How do you feel you did with making other people happy in the last phase? Did you notice that making other people happy had the power to increase how you were feeling? I encourage you to continue to go out of your way to do things for others that are going to make them happy, even though it is no longer a part of your challenge.

This week's challenge is a little different than the last two weeks. This week your challenge is going to be about change. You've already been working on changing your mindset and your attitude, even if you didn't realize you were. This week we are going to take that one step further.

This challenge is also going to give you a lead into your week four challenge.

Challenge – Phase Three: Your challenge this phase is going to center around making changes. For each day this phase, you are going to make a list of something good that happened, something bad that happened, and something positive that can come from the bad thing that happened. Finding something positive out of a negative is a difficult challenge, but it is an important part of finding success and happiness.

Don't worry; I am not going to send you into this challenge without any education on how you can best find the positive in a negative situation. Here are some tips to help you with this process:

1. Identify Your Emotions – Sometimes this can be a bit of a challenge, especially if it involves something unpleasant. If you can label the emotion you are feeling in a negative situation; you can get a better handle on the situation. This is because you will be able to tell what emotions are skewing your interpretation of the situation.

2. Find A Lesson – Experience has always proven to be the best teacher. There is a lesson in every situation. If you work hard to find the lesson, you are more likely to see the positive in a situation.

3. Look For The Benefit – Sometimes when you find yourself in a negative situation, there is something small that you are going to gain a benefit. This could be something like a free cup of coffee after receiving the wrong order at the coffee shop or trying a new dish when the restaurant ran out of an ingredient that is necessary for your usual. In both situations, you can choose to dwell on the negative aspect of the situation, and indeed, they would seem to be a big deal to some people. However, you also have the choice to focus on the compensation the coffee shop gave you or the fantastic new dish you experienced.

Use these tips to help you change the view of some of your experiences this week from negative to positive.

Day Fifteen

Quote*:* "To create more positive results in your life, replace 'if only' with 'next time'." – Celestine Chua

Affirmation*:* There is a great reason this is unfolding before me now.

Some Things You Should Consider:

Have it made up in your mind that failure is not an option for you. Write it down on sticky notes and post it everywhere in your house. The more you see it, the more you hear it, the more you will feel it and then you will live it. When things get rough it's okay to seek help and assistance from resources that have truly good intentions and will provide as being a great influence in helping you to make the best decision for your situations.

Sometimes we tend to dwell in the past, and the past should be left exactly where it is supposed to be. We should take what we need from the past to help us continue to evolve into the person we are destined to become and learn from the mistakes. This is not always very easy but it is the best thing that you can do for yourself. When we learn to let go and recognize that we are human and being human is not an easy journey but we can do it through perseverance and learning who we really are and accepting things.

When things are not going the way you want them to in your life, think about how you typically respond. If you find that you are often responding in a helpless manner, this quote is exactly what you need to think about. Instead of feeling helpless, consider the things you would do differently if you were in the same situation again.

The affirmation above is great for reminding you that everything happens for a reason. Sometimes good things happen, and sometimes bad things happen. Sometimes that reason is clear and other times it isn't. When you feel like you aren't able to identify the reason that something in your life is happening, repeat this quote to yourself as often as you can until you have been able to find positive reasons for the situation.

Day Sixteen

Quote: "A pessimist sees the difficulty in every opportunity; an optimist sees the opportunity in every difficulty" – Winston Churchill

Affirmation: I can overcome this challenge. This challenge is going to lead to great things for me.

Some Things You Should Consider:

When you come across a troubling situation it's so easy to see the negative and then give way to doubt but you cannot allow for a gloomy situation to override your journey. Optimism is an overall expectation that there is greatness in everything. When you have made it to the top of a hill you feel a sense of gratification which is due to your own endurance and optimism about how great the outcome would be. It is the same kind of approach that you should have when facing obstacles in your life. Once you have overcome something you have the ability to share your optimistic point of view to someone who might be going through the same series of events.

Reading the quote, try to determine if you are more of an optimist or a pessimist. Keep in mind; it is possible to be both an optimist and a pessimist depending on the situation that you find yourself in. The key is to bring awareness to yourself if you see that you are becoming a pessimist when faced with a situation.

Think about the situations that you find yourself to be pessimistic in. In those situations, is it possible for you to find something positive that you can focus on?

When you find yourself in a position that it is hard to see the positive in, use the affirmation above to remind yourself that you can overcome any challenges and challenges are meant to lead you to new opportunities, if you are open to seeing them.

Day Seventeen

Quote: "We become what we think about" – Earl Nightingale

Affirmation: I am capable of seeing the good in every situation. I am defined by the things I choose to think about.

Some Things You Should Consider:

Though this may seem like an impossible thing to consider, when you are faced with a difficult situation it is important to not think about it too much. When we over-think on negative circumstances we are not able to gain full control of the situation and collectively make a good decision about how to go about handling it. Overthinking can be a bad habit and it can lead to minor setbacks that if gone unchecked can become a detrimental characteristic in your life.

People who overthink on situations can develop sleeping problems because their brain is so wound up with multiple thoughts and feelings that it never is given the proper opportunity to settle down and relax. An over-thinker also tends to overanalyze everything that they come in contact with. The over-thinker often takes the saying *reading between the lines* very far. The feeling of having to control everything is not healthy and can drive you a little crazy at times and can cause other health issues if it goes untreated.

If you suffer from overthinking things here are a few things you can add to your daily routine to help:

    - Acknowledge that you are having issues with overthinking every situation.

    - Tone down your mind. You can do this by listening to some relaxation tapes or music (I personally enjoy listening to the White Noise genre)

    - Baking, putting together a puzzle or whatever relaxes and quiets your mind.

    - Take small steps to reset your balance. Since this is a habit it is going to take time to revert from it. It is a transformation.

We have already discussed that your frame of mind is a huge part of what goes on around you, or at least how you perceive it. When considering the quote above, "We become what we think about," think about the strengths you have and the strengths you would like to have. Think about a negative situation you have been in lately, what good was in that situation? Did you gain wisdom, understanding, or insight?

Using the affirmation above, remind yourself that there is good in every situation, regardless of how negative it seems like the time. Negative situations do not have the ability to define you. Choose to see, and focus, on whatever good you can find in a moment, even if it isn't directly related to the situation.

Day Eighteen

Quote*:* "Find a place inside where there's joy, and the joy will burn out the pain" – Joseph Campbell

Affirmation*:* My body is healthy; my mind is brilliant; my soul is tranquil.

Some Things You Should Consider:

There is nothing worse than something taking our joy away… but wait, nothing can just come and take joy, it has to be sacrificed. When we allow things to steal our joy we are hurting ourselves. Just like happiness, joy is an emotion that is personal and direct. No one has the right or should ever be given the privilege to take your joy from you.

Sometimes it can seem as if all the negativity around you is bringing you down and you can't bring yourself above it all. The quote above is a reminder to find the joy that is inside you, regardless of what it is you feel joyous about allowing the joy to outshine the negativity all around you.

When faced with hard times it is important to recollect all your memories of joyous times and allow that to rekindle your joyfulness. When you have joy it should not only be kept in you but also shared. It is the gift that keeps on giving. You never know what will make someone's day, week, or year. By sharing and spreading joy and happiness it surely would make all of our lives a lot easier.

It is my belief that the wealthiest thing to have in life is the ultimate joy. Something that comes only from within yourself, nothing or no one has any role in it. It is just you! The experiences that we go through can be horrible or blissful but if we choose to take the beauty out of it and carry that with us we will always find a center of joy within ourselves.

The affirmation above serves as a reminder that there is always something to be thankful for. Having gratitude for your body, mind, and soul is a great way to show joy and to allow that joy to become your primary focus.

Day Nineteen

Quote*:* "Our greatest weakness lies in giving up. The most certain way to succeed is always to try just one more time." – Thomas A. Edison

Affirmation*:* I see the perfection in all my flaws and all my genius.

Some Things You Should Consider:

Think about the quote above. Can you think of a time that you gave up? What about a situation where you decided to try one more time and that last try was the difference between finding success and being unsuccessful? While it is important to know when to approach a situation from a different angle or to leave a situation and focus your efforts elsewhere, if there is something you truly want the only way you are going to get it is to keep trying.

The definition of perseverance is the steadfastness in doing something despite difficulty or delay in achieving success. When you are faced with difficulty or there is a malfunction in the process of you achieving a goal now is the time to reflect on your definition of perseverance and continue to move forward. Whether by changing your approach or if you should move on to another situation, perseverance is key.

Every part of you is important to who you are. This includes your strengths and your weaknesses. If you try to hide your flaws and only show your strengths, you are not going to be happy, and people aren't going to know you for the real you. Embrace your flaws and weaknesses as a crucial part of your personality. Be honest and upfront with yourself. Use the affirmation above to remind yourself that your flaws aren't necessarily a bad thing, and can be used to your advantage.

When we are knowledgeable about our flaws we then have the capability to go about them in a positive direction for correction. Our flaws and attributes are what makes us unique, some of our flaws can be detrimental to our evolvement and this requires some reflection and admittance in order to change. Our greatest attributes should also be reflected upon because these are the things about us that are positive and keep us at our best, we should never neglect them.

Day Twenty

Quote*:* "Believe that your life is worth living, and your belief will help create the fact" – William James

Affirmation*:* I am worth having good things happen to me. I bring happiness into my life.

Some Things You Should Consider:

Do you genuinely feel that your life is worth living? Do you feel like you are making a significant contribution to society, or at the very least to the people who are closest to you?

At some point in every person's life there is time in our lives where we ask ourselves questions like "What is my purpose?" or "Why am I here?". It is a very difficult to answer a question to which you have no answer to give. Everyone has a reason for being here, though it may seem like a cliché of an answer it is in no doubt that we are here for specific reasons.

Somehow we have confused the "rat race" mentality for truly living. While it is important to provide the necessities to sustain life, there are many materialistic things that hold too much power in our lives. When you free yourself from attachments, be it materialistic or other living things, you are opening yourself to a quality life. When you have so many things you must house them be it externally or internally. It is important to let some things go! You will free yourself slowly and surely. In no way am I saying to give up everything in your life that you have but without the clutter of things, people, and places, you and your dreams can grow and blossom.

By using the affirmation above, you can remind yourself that you are worth having good things happening. No one is inherently deserving of having bad things happen to them. The things that happen to us are the things that we have brought into our lives. Remind yourself that you are worth being happiness and that good things can happen to you too, and then look for those good things to begin happening.

Day Twenty-One

Quote*:* "You can always do more than you think you can" – John Wooden

Affirmation*:* I am capable of accomplishing whatever I set my mind to.

Some Things You Should Consider:

The quote above serves as a reminder that we all tend to undersell ourselves, especially to ourselves. Think about a time when you gave up on something because you felt as though you could do what you had originally set out to do. Or, perhaps a time when you only did the bare minimum because you didn't feel like you could contribute anything extra to a project. Now think about a time when you pushed yourself further than you thought you were capable of being pushed. How did you feel afterward?

Use the affirmation above as often as you can. This is another great affirmation to ensure that you put somewhere that you can see it constantly throughout the day. Reminding yourself that you are capable of accomplishing anything you want to is an important part of learning how to push yourself out of your comfort zone and into a position of learning more about yourself.

The 'Comfort Zone' can be a nice place to be briefly but, it is not intended to be a permanent place of residence. When we become permanently placed in our comfort zone we tend to also become complacent and stagnant. These can be the mortal enemies of growth and development. We should always continue to try new things at least once. These things, of course, should always be harmless and potentially good for us.

There are many things that frighten us, but what is fear? Fear usually comes from a place of ignorance, not understanding something in its organic state. When we fear something we initially put a block on out mind to be open to trying to understand it. Sometimes we miss out on such beautiful experiences, opportunities, and people because of fear. Fear should be conquered and not allowed to become the conqueror. This, of course, is not very easy, there is a lot of back and forth between your decision making and your feelings. However, until you make it a point to atlas try and learn before making concrete decisions about something you are essentially allowing for the fear to overtake you and your process.

When we find that there are circumstances that make us feel scared or uncomfortable it is always a good idea to vent about it. It is not always healthy for the mind, body, or spirit to keep bad emotions inside for too long. You can choose to vent out in any way you like. Taking a wine and art session or going for a run, writing in a journal or maybe just talking it over with a close friend andTaking a wine and art session, going for a run, writing in a journal, or maybe just talking it over with a close friend or family member. When we release things that are troubling us we are lifting a burden and it feels so good!

Day Twenty-Two

Quote*:* "Very little is needed to make a happy life; it is all within yourself, in your way of thinking." – Marcus Aurelius

Affirmation*:* My life is fulfilling and makes me happy.

Some Things You Should Consider:

Realizing that living a simpler life is the most liberating movement that we can give our self is one of the best things that one can experience. It is indeed a journey as you learn that you really don't have to have everything just because it is the newest thing or the latest trend. Being yourself and eliminating the unnecessary things in your life all equals to true liberty.

Try to declutter your life and you will surely find some type of peace and serenity. There are a few things that you can try in order to obtain this:

    1. Everything that you have should have a function or hold some true sentimental value to you.

2. Organization; everything that has a function has a space designated for itself.

3. Take your time on things that you have to accomplish. There is no need to rush through life. When we rush through things then we are bound to make mistakes.

Finding a fulfilling life can be difficult if you don't have any way of exploration. I challenge you to go out and find something that you know absolutely nothing about and when you do, join in. You never know what will spark a new adventure in your life and what can come of it.

You are the master of your happiness. No one can determine whether you are happy except you. You make the choice regarding how you are going to react to a situation. Think about a time when you were in a negative situation, but you remained happy overall and didn't let the situation ruin your entire day or your entire week.

The quote above is one that is great for every person in the world to remember. If you can, place this quote somewhere permanent. Somewhere you are going to see it in the morning when you wake up, throughout the day and again in the evening. Telling yourself that your life is fulfilling is the first step in believing your life is fulfilling.

Success Story – Donna

"What God says you are is more important than what others think of you."

— Lailah Gifty Akita

My name is Donna and I must tell you, I am dead excited about affirmations. I follow the Christian faith and I always had it in my head that affirmations were nothing more than New-Age nonsense but I'm here to tell you that they are not and I have found them so incredibly useful.

Most of us watch the Olympics when it's on the TV. I watched the recent Winter Olympics because it gives me inspiration. I see people who have found true success at what they do, people who compete to be the top of their field, their game. They are incredibly focused on what they are doing and, to get to where they are, they have spent virtually every day working towards their goal, preparing themselves and taking part in all the major competitions and other events that happen along the way. They have succeeded at all these events and now they are at the Olympics, champions.

There is one thing that stands out with these athletes; before they compete in their event, they close their eyes and rehearse what they are going to do in their minds. They visualize themselves skiing down the slope, racing that course; they rehearse the routines that they have done so many times before and they feel their muscles working those movements They see it all happening and that happens because they think about it and they practice repeatedly.

I used to play the violin professionally and would practice for a minimum of 5 hours every single day, as well as taking part in rehearsals. It seemed I would always be preparing myself, practicing for a concert and I always had a deadline to work to. I had a specific goal in mind, either of being the best musician I could be or of joining a violinist group and performing with them. When I wasn't physically practicing, I would be mentally practicing.

Affirmations are the same. I asked myself some questions — "where do I want to be in 5 years?", "how healthy do I want to be?", "How successful do I want to be?" and a whole host of other similar questions. Then I asked myself what I should do NOW to get to where I wanted to be in 5 years' time. I never once said to myself that I couldn't achieve it. Instead, I told myself that to be successful, I needed to certain things, the same way that every successful person does. If a successful person got there by eating food that was raw and living and drinking only green tea, then that is what I had to do. If I wanted the same success I had to do the same things.

My next step was to come up with an action plan, a schedule that included these activities I needed to do on a daily basis. I kept saying to myself the affirmation, "Successful people do ABC and because I am a successful person, I must also do ABC". It really didn't take long for everything to fall into place!

My daily affirmations are extremely simple. I say them every morning and I say them every night before I go to bed. I also say them throughout the day as well. I am fighting a disease called muscular dystrophy so one of my daily affirmations is, "I am a very powerful and strong woman". My spirit and my mind tell me it is true and I know that the more I say this affirmation, the more my cells will understand that it is true. Already, I am able to move in ways that I couldn't do several weeks ago.

One thing I do have to be careful of is thought processes and attitude. It is very easy to get wound up in negative thinking, such as, "I am never going to be well again, I will never make a good marriage/mother/wife, I will never have plenty of money" and things like that. But, by using positive affirmations every day, and pushing the negative ones out of my life, I can truly say that my life has changed so much and all of it for the better.

I can see the changes happening in my mind and I keep an eye on the daily actions that I do to make sure I am continually moving forwards, toward my personal goals and not away from them. I write down small goals that are achievable so that I can see them in black and white. This makes me more likely to do them and I will repeat my positive affirmations, stop negative thoughts from forming and it truly works.

A positive affirmation is saying something to yourself that you deeply believe to be true or what you would like to be true; it is in effect, putting faith into action. If you read a passage in the bible that says, "I want nothing more than to see you prosper and be in health" then it is perfectly fine for your affirmation to be, "I am prosperous and healthy, by my faith."

Chapter 5: Phase Four – Days Twenty-Three Through Thirty

"Keep your thoughts positive, because your thoughts become your words.
Keep your words positive, because your words become your behavior.
Keep your behavior positive, because your behavior becomes your habits.
Keep your habits positive, because your habits become your values.
Keep your values positive, because your values become your destiny." – Mahatma Gandhi

You have made it through the first three phases of this book. Let's take a minute and analyze how your thoughts have changed while you have been reading this book. Consider how much happier you are feeling. Think about your levels of optimism when you are facing a difficult situation. Analyze how easily you are conceding defeat and how much harder you are trying to meet your goals.

Another thing to consider is the challenge back from phase one. Have you still been getting up a little bit earlier in the morning to work on reading and thinking about the quotes and affirmations? Do you feel as though waking up a little bit earlier has become a routine now?

Think about how you feel after reading the quotes and affirmations. Are you finding yourself looking forward to seeing what the next day has in store for you? Consider if your days are feeling more positive after reading your daily quote and affirmation.

This phase is going to be set up a little bit differently than the last three phases were. Over the last twenty-two days, I have given you both the quote and the affirmation for you to think about and apply to your life. While I am still going to give you the quote each day, this week's challenge is going to require you to come up with your affirmations that are more personal to you.

Challenge – Phase Four: Coming up with your affirmations isn't going to be difficult. By coming up with your affirmations, they are going to be more meaningful and powerful in your life and your situation. The reason they are more powerful is that they are personalized to your life and your way of thinking. When you use a personalized affirmation instead of one that is generic and not geared to your specific situation it becomes something that you own and that you know geared towards making your life better. This is going to enable you to feel more connected to the words.

You are not going to be alone in this challenge. Each day I am going to guide you through the process of creating your affirmation, working off the quotes that have been included. I am going to guide you through the creation of the affirmation to be sure that you are creating effective affirmations that are going to genuinely benefit your life. Affirmations that don't benefit you are useless. If at any time you find that a particular affirmation is no longer useful to you, switch it out with something else that is of use to you and your life.

How To Write An Effective Affirmation:

Before we move on and have you writing your affirmations, here is a quick outline of what an effective affirmation needs to contain.

- Write an affirmation that is a positive spin on a negative thought or situation. The language you are using is incredibly important. You want to write an affirmation that is going to resonate with you on a personal level.

- Write in the present tense as often as you can. While writing affirmations in the future tense can be acceptable sometimes, it makes it sound as though it is a goal you are going to reach for in the future instead of something you want to see in your life right now. When you have a goal that you are going to work towards sometime in the future, it is not an effective goal, and the same is true for affirmations.

- Avoid words that elicit judgment. Words like never and always are very strong and judgmental words. You want your affirmation to be gentle and bring relief from judgments.

- Make your affirmations personal. Use the pronouns 'I' and 'My' in your affirmations to raise the level of commitment and belief you are going to have in the affirmation.

- Remember to keep your affirmations realistic and direct.

Day Twenty-Three

Quote*:* "Success is not final; failure is not fatal: it is the courage to continue that counts" – Winston Churchill

Affirmation:

To create your affirmation today, think of something that you are currently working on that you feel as though you should quit. This can be something big like a job or relationship, or it could be something small like a goal to go to the gym or read a different book each month. Choose something that you feel like you aren't successful at, but you also don't want to quit. Avoid choosing something like smoking, as that isn't going to fit into this style of affirmation.

The definition of enduring is continuing or long-lasting. The definition of endurance is the fact or power of enduring an unpleasant or difficult process or situation without giving way. We all must have the will to have endurance through hard times. Without endurance there is no progression, and if there is no progression, there is no ultimate recovery.

When you face having to endure a difficult position in life there are a few ways that you can try and abide by:

- Remember that suffering is only temporary and is only as temporary or permanent as one makes it.

- Understand that you cannot fix everything all at one time and that some things are momentarily out of your control.

- Be mindful of how you allow others to influence your decisions. Not everyone has knowledgeable or good intentions on your situation. Even some close friends or families who might have gone through similar things may not be the best to gain insight from. Remember that everyone goes through and handles things differently because we are all unique. What might work for one may not work for you.

Think back over some of the affirmations that you have used over the last few weeks. Many of them had a similar theme to them but were not personal to your situation. Instead, they were generic and able to be used by many different people in different situations.

Write one that is personal to the situation you chose above.

I am going to provide you with some examples as we go through this chapter and for each one I am going to relate them to a runner who is very committed to becoming a better runner but is thinking about giving up because he hasn't successfully run five miles. An example of his affirmation could be: "I am strong enough to go to the gym. I have the stamina to run five miles."

Remember to use only positive words. Using something like "I am not too tired to go to the gym" is not going to be as effective as "I have the energy to go to the gym." Replace any negative words and thoughts with something positive and reassuring.

Day Twenty-Four

Quote: "Getting over a painful experience is much like crossing monkey bars. You have to let go at some point to move forward." – Clive S. Lewis

Affirmation:

We have all gone through painful experiences in our lifetime. Sometimes we can let them go and move on and other times we hold onto those things and let them determine where our lives are going.

Think about something you failed at that you haven't tried to do again because you failed. This can be as big or small as you would like it to be. Remember, starting with something that is small and insignificant isn't going to produce the same results as starting with something meaningful.

Here is an example using the runner I used yesterday. Let's say our runner went to the gym and practiced every day and signed up for a five-mile marathon, but after four miles broke his ankle in three places and needed a lot of rehabilitation before he could even attempt to walk again, never mind run. He could give up on running, which would be easy. Or, he could use an affirmation like this: "My body is strong. I will begin running again."

Using an affirmation like this is going to out the runner into the mindset not to give up and to let go of the fall he had and keep focusing on moving forwards.

Just like yesterday, keep the affirmation positive and don't use any words that have a negative connotation. Negative words tend to stick in your brain as negative words, even if used in a positive way.

When we go through a painful event in our lives we can use that circumstance to help discover or re-discover who we are. There are so many instances where we can learn from reflecting on a loss, traumatic experience or an accident from the past. Although going through the healing process can be a very hard and painful time but it is necessary if you are going to grow. Through that process, we often find the chance to gain self-discovery and resolution.

What are some things you have learned and or gained from a painful event in your life? How has this changed the way that you view life? Have you found any closure or is this painfulness still in control of your everyday life?

We must all go through the process of gaining closure. Closure is absolutely necessary when desiring to move on from a certain situation.

These situations don't necessarily have to be negative but the majority of people are seeking closure from hurtful events in their lives. Just like a physical scar we can carry emotional scars and like any type of physical wound, it takes time to heal. So it is from an emotional wound.

When you have reached closure of something you have made peace and understanding with it. You know that it happened, recognized that it took place, understand that it cannot be changed and that it is what it is. Acceptance of what has taken place and the drive to move forward is all a part of what true closure is. There isn't an easy way to find closure, just like a snowflake, everyone's approach to gaining closure is different from the next ones. After acceptance then comes the of origin of healing and eventually being able to move forward.

Day Twenty-Five

Quote: "Life's most persistent and urgent question is, 'what are you doing for others?" – Martin Luther King, Jr.

Affirmation:

A couple of phases ago, your challenge was to spread happiness to at least one person every day. Were you successful in that challenge? Did you continue going out of your way to make people happy as the days progressed? Today's affirmation is going to be about what you do for the people around you on a regular basis. Consider how much you donate. Whether it is donating your time volunteering, your money or your old belongings, do you believe you are doing everything you can do to help other people?

We are going to use the same runner that we have been using previously for our examples. We know that he is a good runner, and now he wants to help people out with his skills. His affirmation may look something like this: "I can raise awareness of safety while running." Or "I am going to talk to people about overcoming obstacles and not giving up on themselves." This demonstrates that the runner is using his experiences to educate others.

Think about things you can do that would help someone else. It's okay to go out of your way for another person. This affirmation doesn't need to be as specific as "I am going to help Susie with her homework." It can be something like "I am going to donate my time to [a cause that is important to you)" Remember, don't just say it. Act on your affirmation as well. Following through on your affirmation is just as important as creating your affirmation.

There is a great beauty behind helping others. You are creating something meaningful in another person's life. There's no rule to being kind other that you doing something out of pure dedication and from a place of love. Doing something without seeking anything in return is my definition of kindness. There is a difference in having providing a service for someone 'just because' and providing a service for someone to gain validity. When we seek validation from something that was supposed to be done from the heart we are opening up ourselves to disappointment. The disappointment comes from when we are expecting to get rewarded for being kind and then it never comes.

One of the biggest secrets to being happy is by giving to others. Being charitable. Being proactive for a great cause. You don't have to know or be personally close with an individual to give the never ending gift of kindness.

For those who are wondering "Why should I give to others?'" there are many reasons:

- You can begin to fill that emptiness you may have and gain a feeling of meaningfulness for yourself as well as others.

- Serving other people can create a domino effect that never seems to end.

- Helping others can help you grow into a person with strong leadership skills.

If you are not sure where to start being kind here are a few suggestions:

-Volunteer! Volunteer! Volunteer! There are so many groups and organizations that host several opportunities to give to the local communities that you are surrounded by. This is a great way to begin understanding how to give without expecting anything in return. You can gain valuable life experiences and skills. Learn something new about yourself and the cause that you are volunteering for. Most importantly you are doing something for the good of someone or something else.

- Donation. This is a wonderful way to show kindness. That t-shirt that's sitting around collecting dust, or that old set of dinnerware that's in the attic are examples of things that can be given to a person or family that is in true need. There are even community activism groups that take donations from anonymous givers if you are a little on the shy side.

-Share some kind words. If you like someone's hairstyle or their smile, tell them. Our words and the way that we use them have such an impact on the people around us and also ourselves.

-Homemade Gifts! If you are artistically inclined then I employ you to get creative and make something by hand. There are so many people who greatly appreciate the fact of someone taking time to actually make something to show appreciation and kindness for that individual. A candle, a wreath, a photo album, or maybe even some baked goods are all wonderful ideas of things to make for someone else.

Remember: It is always better to give than to receive.

Day Twenty-Six

Quote: "Do not dwell in the past, do not dream of the future, concentrate the mind on the present moment" – Buddha

Affirmation:

Do you know what it means to be mindful? Being mindful means that you are present in each moment. Living in the now. The quote above sums it up completely, —avoid dwelling on the past and the future and focus on the present moment that you are living. Notice all the small things that are happening around. Don't get so caught up in thinking about how your day at work was, or the project that you have due tomorrow that you miss all the little things going on at this moment.

Think about your personal life. Where do your thoughts tend to dwell? Consider if you are constantly stuck in the past or if you are more concerned about where your future is going to bring you. Does this action result in you becoming withdrawn or dislocated from your relationships and interactions with others?

Our runner is focused on running in the next marathon. Because of this focus, he tends to forget his commitments to his family, and this creates a lot of tension. Some of his affirmations may include:

- "I have the focus to be present in the moment."
- "The future will take care of itself. My family is more important than running."
- "I can be present in the moment and be a good runner."

Think about people who are close to you that may feel as though you are always distracted. If this affirmation is harder to write up, consider asking those who are closest to you if they feel like you give them your undivided attention. In personal relationships, this is very important. If your loved ones feel like you are constantly unavailable and inattentive, even when you are physically present, then that can become a serious problem within the relationship that needs to be resolved as soon as possible. When we hurt the ones who truly love us we are not only damaging them but we are in all actuality hurting ourselves as well. Many of us are fortunate to have at least one supporter, if not many in our lives and we should take care not to tarnish that relationship. They can turn out to be one of our greatest inspirations in achieving a goal.

Day Twenty-Seven

Quote*:* "In the long run the pessimist may be proved right, but the optimist has a better time on the trip." – Daniel L. Reardon

Affirmation*:*

We have spent a lot of time analyzing optimism and pessimism, and you should be able to identify which of the two categories you fall into. We have also looked at a couple of different quotes about enjoying the moment instead of focusing on only where we want to go. While that is the focus of this quote, I want you to take your affirmation in a slightly different direction.

Last week your challenge was to make a list of negative situations and something positive that came out of it. Today you are going to come up with three things about yourself that you don't like, and you are going to spin them into positive affirmations.

For example; Our runner suffers from insomnia, he feels that he is always snapping at his children, and he never makes time for his wife. His affirmations would look like this:

- "I am completely free from insomnia," While this isn't yet true, by telling himself repeatedly that it is true, he is going to bring the relief from insomnia into his life.

- "It is deeply satisfying for me to respond with wisdom, love, firmness, and self-control when my children misbehave," By reminding himself how he should respond to his children, he is more likely to respond the way he wants to.

- "It is important to me to spend time with my wife daily. I love my wife and want to see her happy." Using this affirmation is going to make his wife more important to our runner and is going to make spending time with her a priority.

Remember: We are what we think.

Come up with three or more affirmations for yourself that are specific to things about you or your life that you are unhappy with. Try to make these three affirmations ones that you would want to be saying every day.

Day Twenty-Eight

Quote: "To change your life, you have to change yourself. To change yourself you have to change your mindset." – Wilson Kanadi

Affirmation:

We all know that change is not an easy thing to accept, especially once we have been conditioned into a normalcy. Change can often be frightening, positive, slow, gainful, disciplinary, and repetitive. Changing your mindset is not an easy thing to do, but if you want to see some real changes in your life, you need to change how you are looking at things. Our view on situations and how we handle them are mirrored reflection of how our thought processes operate. Many people have many different ways on how to go about facing a situation or changing a problem. Though the flexibility of the multiple ways you can attempt to rectify a situation on you know what will and won't work for you. As we are coming to the end of our thirty days together, it is vital that you can keep up the changes that you have begun making. That is the purpose behind today's affirmation.

To create today's affirmation, you are going to consider what your biggest obstacles in doing the challenges in this book have been. Perhaps you have struggled with making time each day to sit and read and think about the quote and affirmation. Maybe you found that you had a hard time saying the affirmations out loud and believing in them. Or, perhaps it was acknowledging your flaws that you have the hardest time with. Whatever it was that you had a hard time with, use all the knowledge you have about affirmations to create an affirmation to counter whatever your biggest struggle may be.

When we begin to evolve trough the act of change it must be protected. A new way of doing things are as fragile as making a soufflé and can fall through the cracks if precaution of management isn't taken into account. One way to do this is to have control of what surrounds you. What goes on in your environment plays a huge role in how you respond to stimuli. It helps to keep a note of what triggers in your environment, both good and bad, play a role in how you are changing. If you find that there are some things that are hindering your growth then you should find new tactics on how to dismiss it from your life. However, if there are good things that help you when changing these things should be increased in any way possible.

Remember that change is a process. A process that usually takes some time, although there is no logically acclaimed amount of time that it takes to reach the conclusion of that journey called change, it is safe to say that it does not always happen overnight. It's okay to divide goals and aspirations into smaller missions. Be patient with yourself and don't rush. This helps you to keep track of how far you have come and how much more you have to go. It allows you to notice the good and the bad of what has had to happen to allow you to reach your milestone. When you focus on these small successes this builds so much great self-esteem and drive that will keep you moving forward.

Don't forget to reward yourself on reaching these small goals. Treat yourself! Remember that you are what's important here and when you achieve a goal it's perfectly okay to reward yourself with something good, healthy, and beneficial. A trip to the spa, or a night out with the fellas to celebrate, a slice of cake from your favorite bakery, or that new outfit you've had your eye on. These treats can help keep you motivated as you continue to change.

Day Twenty-Nine

Quote: "Most of the important things in the world have been accomplished by people who had kept on trying when there seemed no hope at all." – Dale Carnegie

Affirmation:

Sometimes we hit a point in our lives where things seem hopeless. Chances are, you have been there before, and you will experience that again. Today we are going to create an affirmation for a time when things are feeling hopeless. Even if you aren't in a hopeless situation right now, it is important to have an affirmation that is going to allow you to boost yourself up. This is both to avoid a hopeless situation and to help you out of it if you find yourself in a hopeless situation.

When we begin to feel hopeless in a situation this can affect our day to day activities. We can begin to show the onset signs of depression, isolation, avoidance and not being engaging with others. When you are feeling hopeless you question yourself if something is really worth it or if it is just a waste of time. This is the moment when you must remember that "we are what we think," when you think negatively then you are directing that type of energy into your situation.

When confronting the feeling of hopelessness the number one thing I can think of doing first is trying something new. The beauty of trying something new is it is in a foreign world. Trying something new encourages us to be courageous, open-minded, adventurous, and inquisitive. These are all wonderful attributes to have going through life. You never know where your next inspiration may come from so it's important to venture out and try new things when you have feelings of hopelessness.

Think about a time when you have felt hopeless in the past. What is something someone said to you that helped you, or something you wish someone had said to you?

We are going to go back to our runner to demonstrate an example. Our runner is getting ready to run an eight-mile marathon. The marathon states that the eight miles must be completed in forty minutes to earn a medal. Our runner desperately wants this medal, but the best time he can get is fifty minutes, and he feels hopeless. Here are a couple of affirmations he could use:

- "I can run eight miles in forty minutes."
- "I am a successful runner; I have earned my times."
- "My family loves me, and I am a great person just the way I am."

As you can see, the third example is a little more generic than the first two. While you want to be as specific as possible, sometimes an affirmation that leans towards being generic is helpful as you can apply it to more aspects of your life. If this is an affirmation you are going to keep in your reserves for when you need it, a generic affirmation can be altered to match a situation later, when the situation presents itself.

Day Thirty

Quote: "Why Worry? If you've done the very best you can, worrying won't make it any better" – Walt Disney

Affirmation:

Knowing that you have done the best you can in any situation is an important part of being at peace with the decisions you have made and the outcomes of those decisions. As we end this book, you may be worried about moving into using affirmations on your own. Don't be. By doing the best you could throughout this book, you have undergone a transformation in your thinking, and you are now ready to move forward on your own.

Worrying can have a direct effect on our physical health; causing headaches, gastrointestinal complications, anxiety, sleep disruptions, hormone imbalances, and much more...

When facing worry we have to realize that it is an emotion and an emotion that is defined as a natural instinctive state of mind which comes from a person's circumstances. In other words, it's totally natural to worry about something at one point or another. However, when you allow this worry to take over your life you are opening yourself to potentially becoming dysfunctional and in a monotonous routine.

Worrying about what is going to happen next is something that we are all guilty of, but doesn't accomplish anything. Instead of requiring you to create your affirmation today, I am going to give you five affirmations that are about not worrying. I want you to read through them and choose the one that you feel is the most natural for you to say. Take this affirmation and change the words to make it personal and about you.

- "I am letting go of my worries."
- "I am able to solve problems and worries using logic."
- "I will be relaxed and calm."
- "I am a naturally calm person."
- "I am confident and at peace with my life right now."

Success Story – Karen

"If you are determined to achieve your dreams, you must be ready to accept and affirm positive things about yourself. Affirm positively! Say positive things and encourage yourself that you can make it." – Israelmore Ayivor

My name is Karen and I want to tell you about my personal experience with affirmations. Recently, I learned a great deal about using affirmations to lose weight, about how it worked and now I want to share my experiences with you.

My whole life has been about one big search. I always had it in my mind that there was something terribly important that we had all forgotten, something about living how we do on earth and I have always believed that we the human race, are far powerful than we ever knew.

One way or another, I have been on this diet or that one ever since I was a teenager. I am now in my middle fifties. When I diet these days, no matter what I do, no matter how much I restrict what I eat, nothing happens. I can, however, put weight on easily when I eat normally.

I decided that I needed to change the way I was thinking, to start thinking positive things about losing weight. What else did I have to lose? Diets weren't working anymore so the very first thing I thought was that I was never going to go on another diet again. And it is to this that I attribute the success of my affirmations. When you think about it, the act of dieting causes a feeling of lacking. I firmly believe that your unconsciousness believes that you are starving when you go on a diet and, as such, it holds on fast to all that stored fat so that, when you "starve" yourself again, it can feed you and keep you alive. It is also this very thing that causes you to gain every single pound of fat back; it has absolutely no consideration of the good or the bad about losing weight.

Recently, I put on weight, about 8 lbs. so I changed my affirmation. I said to myself, *"I am .... lbs."*. I made it 8 lbs. lower than what I weighed and I said it every single night before I went to bed, as well as every single morning when I got up. However, it was also a mantra that I repeated through the course of the day and during the night if I woke. Two weeks later, I weighed myself; nothing had changed. After three weeks, those 8 lbs. had disappeared.

When I tried this gain, I lowered my affirmation weight by 10 lbs. and kept repeating my affirmation every day for two months. Nothing happened so I thought it must have been a fluke the first time around. I tried again but this time reducing my weight but just 5 lbs. It did work but it took a month. I tried again with the 5 lbs. reduction but this time, I could repeat the affirmation much more than I could before and it only took two weeks to work this time.

This month, I am concentrating on other things but I will return to my weight loss soon. What is interesting this time is that, no matter what I eat, I have neither gained any weight nor lost it? My unconscious is under the belief that I will weight whatever my last affirmation was, no matter what I do, or until I tell it otherwise.

I hope this will encourage you to give affirmations a try. You do need to be able to stick to it and push on even though you may want to give but it will work; it did for me where nothing else would.

Chapter 6: What if it Doesn't Work?

Muhammad Ali had one affirmation that he used to use repeatedly until he became the words he spoke – *"I AM THE GREATEST"*

Provided they are used properly, affirmations have been scientifically proven to be a truly effective means of becoming who you want to be, the person you must become to achieve all that you want to achieve throughout life. However, affirmations have also been given something of a bad time because many people have tried them and have failed to achieve what they want.

The reason they have failed is because things have changed. For many decades, so-called gurus and experts told us that we should be doing affirmations in a specific way, a way that is destined to be completely ineffective and will only cause failure, no matter how much you try them. There are two problems here:

First off, if you lie to yourself, it simply won't work. Saying things like:

"I am a millionaire" when you clearly aren't

"My body fat is only 7%" when it most certainly isn't

"I have achieved every goal I set for myself in the last year" when you really haven't

All of this is going to fail because you are lying to yourself. This way of saying affirmations, as if you have already achieved something or become something you aren't is the biggest single reason for failure. If you use this technique, every time you speak an affirmation that isn't based firmly in truth, your unconscious will kick it aside because it knows it isn't true. You are an intelligent person and repeatedly lying to yourself will never work simply because the truth will always come out.

Let's take an affirmation like, *"I am a magnet for money; money comes to me in vast amounts without any effort"*; this might make you feel fantastic while you are saying it because it takes away from your very real worries about finances but it will never ever result in income. Anyone who sits and waits for money to come to them without doing anything to make it happen will always be cash poor.

If you want to generate money in abundance, or anything else that you desire, you do have to do something to make it happen. Every action you take must be aligned with the results that you want to achieve and affirmations must both state and affirm both parts of that.

The following are four steps that will help you to create affirmations that you can implement, affirmations that will go into your conscious mind and your subconscious to produce the results that you want for success beyond what you thought possible before.

Each affirmation must be created in this way:

Step 1 – The Result That You Are Committed to Achieving and Why

Note that you are not beginning with something that you WANT. We all want something but we don't always get what we want. Instead, we only get what we are committed to achieving. So you want to be a millionaire; don't we all so come and join this club that is not exclusive. Oh, hold on, you are committed to becoming a millionaire, 100% committed and you will do whatever is necessary, the actions that you need to take to achieve that result. Now, we're on the right track.

Action - write down one very specific and extraordinary result that you are committed to achieving. Choose one that is going to challenge you and will make significant improvements to your life; improvements that you are 100% ready to commit to making. It doesn't matter yet that you don't know how you will achieve this, that will come later. Next, your affirmation must contain a reason why you are going to do this, compelling reasons and the benefit that you will get from it.

Examples

Here are some examples of affirmations written in this way:

" I am committed to increasing my income in the next year from $... to $... so that I can give my family financial security."

"I am committed 100% to losing ...lbs. and weighing ...lbs. by (input a specific date) so that I can set the right example for my children/decrease my risks of serious disease."

Step 2 – The Actions You Commit to Taking and When

It would be easy to write down an affirmation that merely says what you want without saying what you are going to do but this would be as good as pointless. In fact, it could be seen as being counter-productive because all you are doing is telling your subconscious that you can achieve the result without doing anything.

Action – Clarify exactly what you are going to do to achieve the result you want, be it an activity, an action or a habit that needs to be changed if you are going to be successful. State clearly when you will do this and how often you must do to achieve the necessary action.

Examples:

"To ensure that I increase my income, I am 100% committed to making 40 prospecting calls every day, between 8 am and 10 am, no matter what happens.

"To make sure I lose ...lbs., I am committed 100% to attending the gym every day and running for at least 20 minutes a day on the treadmill between 6 am and 7 am".

If you make your actions specific, the better they will be. Make sure that you include how often, how many and specific time frames.

Step 3 – Repeat Your Affirmation Each Morning with Emotion

Remember this; these affirmations are designed purely to make you feel better. These are statements that you have written, statements that have been engineered to program your mindset and beliefs into your subconscious so that you can achieve the outcome you want. At the same time, they will be telling your conscious mind that you need to remain focused on high priorities and carry out the actions that are going to get you to the end of your journey.

That said, if your affirmations are going to be effective, you must use emotion when you are saying them. If you repeat your affirmation over and over without feeling the truth of it, it won't work or at best, you will only get mediocre results. It is your responsibility to generate real excitement and real determination and then bring those emotions into each of your affirmations, every time you say them.

Action – Set a specific time every morning to say your affirmations. The reason for this is because you have to both program the subconscious and train the conscious mind on what is truly important to you and what your commitments are to making it happen. To do this, you must be consistent and so you have to say your affirmations at the same time every single day. Once you make these a solid part of your routine, only then will you see the results start to happen.

Step 4 – Update Your Affirmations and Evolve Them Constantly

As your commitments begin to be realized, you will improve and evolve and, because of that, your affirmations must do the same. Once you reach a goal, set up a new one and add it to your affirmation. You can have an affirmation for every part of your life that is significant – your health, finances, family, relationships, etc. – and you should evolve your affirmations on a constant basis as your learning increases.

In the next few chapters, I am going to give you some positive affirmations to say for three different areas of your life – success, health, and career, followed by some motivational ones and then I will be showing you some techniques on learning how to write and use your own affirmations. Once you have completed the 30-day course, don't stop. Continue to make these affirmations a part of your daily routine. Pick any of these affirmations or write your own and continue reaping the success that you have already experienced.

Chapter 7: Positive Affirmations for Success

Breathe in deeply a couple of times and clear out your mind – you do not need any distractions at this point. When you read these affirmations, read them with true meaning and really feel the meaning of each one deep inside of you. Repeat each one as many times as necessary until you really feel it, in your bones and in your heart.

Smile widely and make it a genuine smile and then read each of them aloud. If you need help in truly feeling the power of each one, don't be afraid to jump up and down, grab at the air and use your fists to pull that energy into you. Repeat them with real deep meaning to bring much faster results. This is the trick with affirmations – you must mean them and you have to feel them.

I am always present and I am always in the moment.

I am open to receiving great quantities wealth, health, and happiness.

My life is mine to create.

I enjoy my life. It is full of beauty and abundance.

I attract everything I need to be happy, whole and healthy and I do it effortlessly.

I am consistently finding new opportunities and successes.

I live my life wholeheartedly and with passion.

My world is filled with love, beauty, happiness, and abundance.

I deserve prosperity and abundance.

I use my unique talents and gifts to manifest abundance.

I live a life full of joy and honesty.

I deserve to live a full and complete life.

I produce financial affluence by doing what I love and loving what I do.

I am surrounded by people who love me and give me support.

People recognize my existence and they appreciate it.

My love and pure zest for life motivate and inspire other people.

I share my gifts with other people generously and I accept their gifts with genuine gratitude.

I am known for my full-of-life attitude and the positive energy I give off.

I seek mentorship and inspiration from successful people that I admire.

I listen with patience, understanding, and compassion to other people.

I communicate professionally, gracefully and clearly.

My success is vital.

I contribute an influential and positive presence to the world.

I celebrate life and the beauty of it every single day.

I live a full life.

I create the lifestyle I want to live with enthusiasm.

I choose success, happiness, and health.

I celebrate love, health, and life itself every day.

The miracle and magic of life surround me wherever I go!

Right now, every dream I have is coming true!

And so it is.

Chapter 8: Positive Affirmations for Good Health

When you are healthy you are wealthy and positive affirmations play a huge part in this. When your mind is centered around thoughts of health, your body will follow and will be healthier. We know that there is a connection between the mind and the body and it has been agreed that some diseases are psychosomatic – caused by emotion and thought.

Even those diseases that are caused by a germ can be thought of in some way as being psychosomatic because we "allow" the germs to enter our bodies or germs that already exist there will become stronger, strong enough to cause a disease simply because your immune system is not working effectively because of emotion.

All emotion is controlled completely by thought and we all know that thought can be formed entirely at will. Positive affirmations will help to mold those thoughts and that is where the connection between these affirmations and your health become clearer.

There is an old saying, *"Change Your Thoughts, Change Your Life"* and it is perfectly possible to fill up your mind with thoughts of health just by using the right positive affirmations. Repeating them over and over again will train your subconscious mind to the extent where it begins to transform your body in line with your thoughts.

Believe it or now, and I would never make light of a subject like this, there have been cases of cancer being overcome by the power of thought. You all know about placebos and it is well known that in medical terms, the placebo effect is psychological, i.e. in your mind. A patient would be given a sugar pill instead of the real medication but would be told that it was the real thing needed to cure his condition. And in many cases, it will cure it because the patient is convinced he is taking the proper medication the placebo itself does nothing; it is all in his mind. Affirmations can have the same effect on your body.

There is also evidence that different mental emotions cause different chemicals to be produced in your body. When you are feeling happy, the chemicals produced are beneficial to your body. When you are feeling sad, those chemicals are harmful to your body. As such, your thoughts affect what your body feels and does. It is very clear that positive affirmations can have very positive health effects on your body.

Below is a list of health affirmations. Choose only those that fit your situation and repeat 100 times every day for a period of 6 months. If you are on any medication that has been prescribed for your condition, DO NOT, under any circumstances, stop taking it. Affirmations are designed as a way of complementing the medication, not replacing it, and they will help to strengthen your mind, change your thought direction and assist your body in healing.

Every single day, in every single way, I am getting better and healthier

I love myself and I am healthy

Every single cell throughout my body is conscious of health. I am a health nut

My mind is perfectly calm and full of peace and my body is full of vitality and energy

I don't eat junk; I eat nutritious healthy food that is beneficial to my body and I drink large quantities of water to cleanse my system

I only think positive thoughts and I am always joyful and happy, no matter what life throws at me

I always feel great and my body feels great; I radiate positivity and happiness

Every single day is a brand-new day of health, happiness, and hope

It is my birthright to be healthy. I take good care of my body and I bless it daily

I am always happy, hearty and hale. Happy in spirit, hearty in disposition and hale in body

My heart is strong and my body is steel. I am full of energy, vitality and am vigorous

Godliness is first, good health is second. I possess a healthy body and a healthy mind

With each day that passes, my body becomes healthier and full of energy

My body is a temple. It is clean, holy and good

I practice deep breathing, take regular exercise and only eat healthy nutritious foods

I am free of high/low blood pressure, I am free of diabetes and am free of any other disease that may threaten my life

I release any ill feelings I have, about anything or anyone and I forgive everyone that is associated with me

Every day, I thank God and I thank everybody in my life. I know that, without you all, I am not a complete person and I thank you for coming into and for staying in my life

My Motto is "Healthy, wealthy and wise". I have a healthy body, I have wealth and I have a wise mind

I am my creator. I am the one, I am the All

Chapter 9: Positive Affirmations for your Career

The positive career affirmations I am going to tell you will help you to see your goals, your career, your attitude and your relationships with everyone you work with or for more clearly. The definition of a career is, "a chosen pursuit, a profession or an occupation; the general course or progression of one's working life or one's professional achievements".

It is perfectly natural to want a successful career in the job or area that you choose and we all want to do a good job, to enjoy it and to earn enough money. You can choose a career in a specific job, in a specific profession or a business and it is perfectly possible to earn job satisfaction and a good reward in financial terms in any of these three areas, provided you are prepared to take the right steps necessary to ensure it.

There are lots of important things, not least knowledge in your chosen field, hard work, and proper planning, not to mention a real vision. However, more important is having the right attitude mentally. Thomas Jefferson once said, *nothing can stop the man with the right mental attitude from achieving his goal; nothing on earth can help the man with the wrong mental attitude."*

At times, we all need a good boost mentally in our work; we sometimes need to give ourselves a good talking to and this is where positive career affirmations can help you immensely. The affirmations I have listed below are going to help you get in tune with the work you do, in turn with your colleagues, your bosses, and your juniors. They will help you to get your priorities in the right order and help to focus your mind on your career.

Pick one or more from this list. You can use them on their own or you can combine them to make your own affirmations that suit your circumstances. Repeat your affirmations 100 times a day as a minimum, standing in front of a mirror as you say them. Over time, your mindset will change and you will become more successful in your career.

At this moment, I am working in the job of my dreams

I love my career; I get total job satisfaction from it

I love my career; It lets me grow and gives me good financial reward

I can balance my family and my career so that they work together

I am valued at my place of work and I am always listened to respectfully

I have a good relationship with my boss and all my colleagues

I am content because the work I do doesn't just benefit me; it also benefits the society that I live in

My job has fantastic career prospects, opportunities for promotion and great financial compensation

Because I have such a positive attitude mentally, I always get the best projects and the best people to help me with them

I am always full of enthusiasm and this rubs off on my colleagues, resulting in a fantastic and productive working day for everyone

I was born to be an entrepreneur. Whenever opportunities arise, I recognize then and I seize them

I am a master at sales. My customers trust me and they love me and my order book is always full to overflowing

I have a work ethic that makes sure I always get the pay raises and the promotions

My forte is my self-discipline. In my home, my family comes first and in my workplace, work comes first

I always take responsibility for my work and my actions. My work motto is, "The buck stops here".

I practice diligence in my work, honesty in my attitude and have a positive mindset at all times which opens up new opportunities for me

I look after my junior staff and I help them in the appropriate way. I am friendly toward my colleagues and show respect to my seniors

To me, a career is just the means to the end. The end is the total fulfillment of my true potential and happiness and my career gives me that every day.

I do my very best in my career every single day and I give everything with no reservations. The fruits of that labor taste very sweet

My one aim is to satisfy my customers and I always give everything to be the best that I can be and to achieve that aim

Chapter 10: Positive Affirmations for Motivation

No matter what you do in life, the most important thing is motivation. Positive motivational affirmations will give you the strength that you need to start any task and see it right through to completion. It is the motivation that allows you start that task or start any action that is needed to help you reach your goal. Without that motivation, you may start out with all the best intentions but they will soon wither away and you will give up or only do a half-hearted job.

Think of motivation as the protein that builds up the muscles and as the carbohydrate that fuels you with the energy you need to complete the task that takes you to your goal. Positive affirmations are fuel; the feed the actions and, while you can start a job or a task without any motivation, you need it to finish Repeating these affirmations regularly will provide you with an inner sense of motivation, an urge to get on and do what must be done without any pushing and prompting, from you or from others. Your actions will be on a kind of auto-pilot until your goal is reached.

There is evidence from studies that finds we radiate those thoughts that are in our minds the most often. In turn, those thoughts will attract to you the circumstances that favor those thoughts and favor the people around you who have similar thoughts. Throughout this book, I have given you several quotes – don't underestimate the importance of these. They are an important resource for motivation because they tend to contain pearls of wisdom from people who are successful, whose words come from their life experiences. That makes them invaluable because there is no better teacher than life itself.

Like every other type of affirmation, a motivational affirmation is simple to prepare. Simply think about the task you are going to do and take note of the positive thoughts that enter your mind. Formulate those thoughts and include them in your affirmations, like the following examples:

I can! I can do it! I can!

When I have clear intentions, the universe will cooperate with me and I can do anything

I think only positive thoughts and only positive things are happening in my life

I am one of life's go-getters and I will do anything to achieve my goals

Success is my middle name. I am successful at everything I do

The doors that lead to opportunity are always open and I take full advantage of them with no exception

Motivation comes easily and quickly to me and I can motivate others

I am filled with hope and with energy and I live my life fully

I love challenges and I face them head on and win

Motivation is inside of me; I motivate myself

My only option in life is success. I push forward and I succeed

I make a difference to other people and I try to help them to the best of my ability

My ultimate goal is motivation. I only see the goal until I get to it

I know what my worth is and I know that I deserve success; I get success

My work is a true motivator and I will not stop until I achieve my goal

I love life; it is fulfilling and it is beautiful

Chapter 11: Preparing and Using Your Own Affirmations

So, you now know that, if you want to change your beliefs and make a new reality for yourself, you must constantly bombard your mind, conscious and subconscious, with the thoughts of what you truly desire. However, it is very important that you word these thoughts carefully otherwise, you may not get the results that you are looking for. As such, there are several things that you must do, or not do as the case may be, to get the best result out of your affirmations. I already mentioned some of these earlier but, as with affirmations, it doesn't hurt to repeat things!

- ☐ Always do your affirmations in the present tense. The past is gone and cannot be changed. Using the future tense simply tells your mind that you will do something in the future, not that you are doing it now.

Your subconscious mind will always try, very literally, to do what is asked of it. As such, you should say things like, "I am rich", "I have wealth beyond belief", I am ready to be rich and to prosper", or "II choose to be prosperous"

Psychologists say that using the term "choose" is far better because then it becomes your choice. Bear in mind one thing that is very true – what your life is now is because of choices that you have made in the past

- ☐ Always be positive because only a positive affirmation will truly work

The subconscious mind struggles to deal with negatives so if you were to say something like, "I am not overweight", by the time it reaches your subconscious, the word "not" has been removed or is ignored and that statement turns into "I am overweight".

What really happens comes down to a law we call "Focus and Growth". By this law, whatever you truly focus on will grow. So, when you say to yourself, "I am not overweight", the focus is firmly on "overweight". Your subconscious mind concentrates all its efforts on keeping you or making you overweight so it is far better to say something like, "I am slim and fit" or, "I weigh … kgs/lbs.".

- ☐ Positive affirmations can be written down or they can be spoken

When you speak your positive affirmations out loud, say them emphatically, throughout the course of the day. At the very least, what you should be doing is saying each one twenty times every morning, when you get up and then twenty times before you go to bed. This will fix that affirmation into your mind. Even better, say them 100 times a day. The more you can repeat them, the better the result will be.

If you choose to write your affirmations, write each one down at least fifteen times a day. Writing is the fastest way to impress something into your subconscious mind. Have you ever heard of Scott Adams? He is a world-famous cartoonist, known for "Dilbert" and he is the perfect example of how important written affirmations are. Go find some "Dilbert" and you will see exactly what I mean. Then we have the Mirror technique, which I will tell you more about in a short while.

☐ Repetition is vital.

If you really want your life to change significantly in any way, your affirmations must be repeated through the day. In time, the more you repeat them, they will become a reality to you and not just words. If you were to do them for just a few days, you shouldn't expect to see the results that you want. You must be like a dog with a bone; keep on going at them until you have achieved your goals.

There is an old story that demonstrates this:

There are two villages, side by side, A and B. Both villages always suffered from a shortage of water. The village called A suddenly discovered a rain dance that they performed and it rained. When they saw this, the village called B also did this rain dance but they never got any rain. They did it a few times, still, no rain fell. In the end, the chief of B went to see the chief of A to ask him for some help. The chief of A simply said to him, "we do this dance until the rains come; we don't do the dance and stop, expecting it to happen"

The same applies to your affirmations – do them and do them continually until you get the result you desire.

The Mirror Technique

One of the best methods for doing positive affirmations is the Mirror Technique and it has been used by many of the greatest authors of self-help books. Here is how to do it:

Stand before your mirror and look deeply into your own eyes. Repeat your affirmations with total gusto and enthusiasm. Fill them with energy. When you look into your own eyes, you will find it much easier to make the connection with your subconscious mind

You must do this regularly. In fact, whenever you are in your own home and you walk past a mirror of any description, stop, consider it, into your eyes and repeat those affirmations several times. This is an incredibly powerful technique and I guarantee you that, done regularly, it will work

The Card Technique

This is another well-known technique and here's how it's done:

Take a piece of card, 3" by 5", or a size that fits into your wallet or your pocket. On it, write your chosen affirmation in large bold lettering. Look at this card frequently throughout the day. It doesn't matter where you are; you can easily whip the card out, read it and then put it back. Don't show it to anyone and don't tell anyone what you are doing because sharing it with others will eliminate all the energy that you have put into the affirmation. Do try and look at the card at least ten times a day, if not more. The more you do it, the more chance there is of your subconscious mind getting to work quicker and bringing about your desires.

Affirmations have been of huge help to thousands upon thousands of people across the world, helping to bring about significant changes, changes that they truly want to happen. But they don't seem to work for everyone so, how can these powerful things bring success for one but fail completely for another?

Affirmations will work to program your subconscious into believing what you are stating. The simple reason for this is, your mind has no idea of the difference between reality and fantasy. When you watch a movie, for example, and you laugh at something or you cry, your mind is displaying empathy with the situation and the characters on the screen, even though it isn't real.

There are two types of affirmation – positive and negative. Most of us can, no doubt, go back to our childhoods and can remember being told that we couldn't do something, we didn't have the ability necessary, whether we were told it by a parent, a teacher, even a coach or a friend. They might have told you that were clumsy or fat. These statements stay with you for life. They hide either in your subconscious or conscious mind, and they will be reinforced throughout your entire life – unless you do something to stop them.

According to the Grandfather of Psychology of the Self, Heinz Kohut, fear of failing is more often than not connected to a fear we had in childhood of being abandoned, be it emotionally or physically. When you are afraid of failure, you will automatically overestimate the risks that you are taking and you will always come up with the absolute worst-case scenario. This is the emotional twin of the fear of being abandoned. You will go out of your way to avoid any opportunities that could lead to success and, when you fail, which is inevitable in this case, you are simply reaffirming that negative affirmation, be it something like, "Success will never come to me" or "Success just isn't meant to be in my life".

If that belief has been rooted deeply into your subconscious, it will almost certainly walk all over any positive affirmations, even if you are not aware of it. Therefore positive affirmations don't always work for everyone – their thought patterns have been strongly afflicted by something negative and this is so strong that it can knock away any positives. That said, you can get over this. There are ways to add strength to a positive affirmation so that it can win over the negative. Here we look at a few suggestions on how to make positive affirmations truly work for you:

5 Steps to Making Positive Affirmations More Powerful and Effective
Step 1

Write down in a list everything that you have always considered to be a negative quality of yours. Make sure that you include criticisms that others have made about you, anything that you may have been holding on to. It doesn't matter what it is – it could be something a friend has said to you recently, something your parents, a teacher or a sibling said to you in your childhood or what your boss said to you in your last performance review.

Make sure that you do not, at this stage, judge whether these statements are accurate and do keep in mind that every single person has flaws, whether they believe it or not.

This is one of the simple beauties of being a human being – just write everything down and then look for common threads. It could be something like, "I'm not worthy". This is a great place to begin making changes in your life, positive changes.

When you write down that belief, the one that recurs throughout your statements, take note of whether you are hanging on to that belief within your body. For example, when you write it down, do you get a feeling of dread in your stomach or your heart? A feeling of tightness? If you do, you must now ask yourself if this concept is productive or helpful to your life. If it isn't, ask yourself what would be.

Step 2

Now you have done this, you can write an affirmation that is based on the positive sides of your self-judgment. Have a thesaurus to hand so that you can find truly powerful words that will help boost your affirmations. Instead of writing, for example, "I am worthy", you could write something along the lines of, "I am a remarkable person and I am cherished:".

Once you have written your affirmation down, ask a close friend to read through it and ask them if they have any suggestions that will make your statement stronger.

Step 3

When you have your affirmation written exactly as you want it, say it aloud for a minimum of 5 minutes at a time, at least three times per day. Go for first thing in the morning, the middle of the day and last thing at night. The best times are when you are having a shave or applying makeup – look in the mirror, straight into your own eyes, and say the positive affirmation out loud.

You could also write it down several times in a notebook as this will help with the reinforcement of that belief into your subconscious. Notice that, as you write it, over the course of time, your writing style will change. This is a big clue as to how your mind is changing, as to how you are perceiving the statement and is a good chart for marking your progression

Step 4

To make sure that your affirmation is firmly anchored in your body, while you are repeating it, put your hand onto the part of your body that felt tight or uncomfortable when you write the negative statement or belief in the first step. For example, if you felt a sinking feeling in your stomach, place your hand over your stomach. Breathe deeply as you say or write your affirmation down. As your mind starts to be reprogrammed, you need to be able to move on from the original concept of that statement to the real and positive feeling of the quality you are looking for.

Step 5

Ask a good friend or a life coach to say your affirmation to you repeatedly. As they are saying, for example, "you are a remarkable person and you are cherished", you must identify that statement as a message that is "good fathering" or "good mothering". If you can't find someone that you trust to help you here, use the mirror technique and use your own reflection to reinforce that message in your mind and body.

Affirmations are incredibly powerful and can help you to change your state of mind, your mood and can help you manifest the changes that you want to bring about in your life. To make them work best, you should first identify the negative belief that is their direct opposite.

If you are finding that these suggestions are still not helping positive affirmations to work for you, it may be that you have deep-seated fears and irrationals that can only be dealt with through the help of a professionally trained therapist. It could be that you are not consciously aware of what it is, it could be buried deeply in your subconscious and must be uncovered if this is to work for you.

Mindfulness meditation is a fantastic tool that can help you to unbury unhealthy thought patterns and helps you to put them into categories, allowing you to properly identify these that are positive and those that are negative or afflicted. Mindfulness is not about changing you; it is about having the power to accept what is and then change to what is possible

Conclusion

Congratulations, you have made it to the end of this book. I hope that as you have read this book, you have found quotes and affirmations that have caused you to dig deep into yourself and find the potential buried inside. Now that you have set the foundation and begun changing your mindset, you are ready to take what you have learned and fill your life with happiness, success, and optimism.

As you move forward, remember to continue saying the affirmations that you feel speak to you the loudest. You don't want to say thirty plus affirmations a day, but choose the ones that most apply to your life and continue saying them daily. Saying affirmations every day has the power to bring great things into your life. Think about all the ways that your life has improved in the last thirty days. You are no longer the person who picked his book up a month ago. You are now more confident and ready to take on the world.

Thank you again for downloading my book, *"Positive Thinking: 30 Days Of Motivation And Affirmations: Change Your "Mindset" & Fill Your Life With Happiness, Success, & Optimism!"* I hope you enjoyed the readings in this book and wish you all the best on your continuing journey.

Help me improve this book

While I have never met you, if you made it through this book I know that you are the kind of person that is wanting to get better and is willing to take on tough feedback to get to that point. You and I are cut from the same cloth in that respect. I am always looking to get better and I wish to not just improve myself, but also this book. If you have positive feedback, please take the time to leave a review. It will help other find this book and it can help change a life in the same way that it changed yours. If you have constructive feedback, please also leave a review. It will help me better understand what you, the reader, need to make significant improvements in your life. I will take your feedback and use it to improve this book so that it can become more powerful and beneficial to all those who encounter it.

REMEMBER TO JOIN THE GROUP NOW!

If you have not joined the Mastermind Self Development group yet, now is your time! You will receive videos and articles from top authorities in self-development as well as a special group only offers on new books and training programs. There will also be a monthly member only draw that gives you a chance to win any book from your Kindle wish list!

If you sign up through this link http://www.mastermindselfdevelopment.com/specialreport you will also get a special free report on the Wheel of Life. This report will give you a visual look at your current life and then take you through a series of exercises that will help you plan what your perfect life looks like. The workbook does not end there; we then take you through a process to help you plan how to achieve that perfect life. The process is very powerful and has the potential to change your life forever. Join the group now and start to change your life! http://www.mastermindselfdevelopment.com/specialreport

Printed in Great Britain
by Amazon